Contents

Dedicated to Steve Jobs

The night it was announced Steve Jobs had passed away, by coincidence my wife and I already had tickets to San Francisco for early the next morning because I was scheduled to speak at a Silicon Valley Code Camp.

After arriving in San Francisco, we drove to Cupertino to make some sense of the loss of a great visionary. The flags at Apple were flying at half-mast and many others had gathered to honor him with candles, flowers, posters and apples.

We drove to the home where Steve created the first Apple computer, then on to the last place he called home in Palo Alto where many others gathered to pay respects and where his silver Mercedes (famously without license plates) still sat in front of his house.

It was there I purposed to write this book series and do for *iOS* app development what Steve had done for users of iOS devices—make app development accessible to the masses of non-programmers, teaching them to create apps that surprise and amaze their users.

iOS ... for

Boo ... S 7

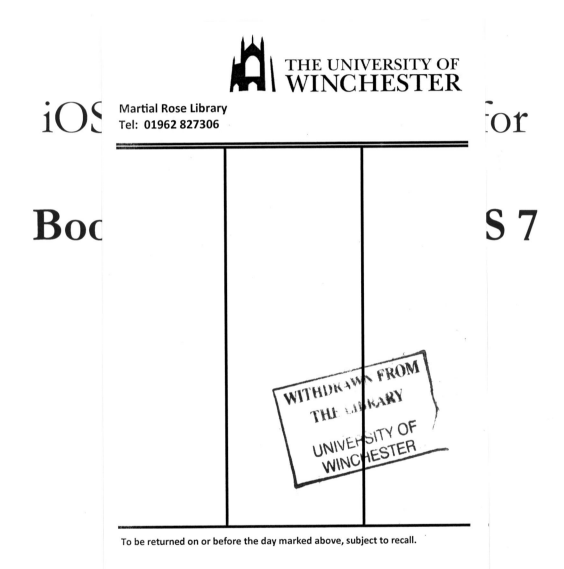

Author

Kevin J McNeish

Technical Editor

Greg Lee

Photography

Sharlene M McNeish

Copy Editor

Benjamin J Miller

© 2013 Oak Leaf Enterprises, Inc.

1716 Union Mills Rd.
Troy, VA 22974
434-979-2417

http://www.iOSAppsForNonProgrammers.com

ISBN: 098823274X
ISBN-13: 978-0-9882327-4-7

Foreword

This book is the first in a series designed to teach non-programmers to create *iOS* apps. Many books designed for beginning iOS app developers assume *way* too much. This book series intends to rectify that by assuming you know *nothing* about programming.

This book is your "easy in." It's designed to build confidence that you really can build apps for the iPhone, iPad and iPod Touch.

Each chapter and exercise has been reviewed by people like you—with little or no experience (mostly "no experience") in creating apps. I rewrote many sections of the book multiple times, added diagrams, and improved examples until all of our "beta readers" completely understood each key concept.

Once you master the concepts in this book, you will be able to move forward and learn other technologies such as the Objective-C programming language, how to create a great user experience, and how to make use of the many tools available in Apple's Software Developer Kit. All of these topics are covered in other books in our *iOS App for Non-Programmers* series, with you, the non-programmer, in mind.

So, buckle up, and let's get started.

Introduction

Whether you are creating apps you sell yourself, or you are creating an app for someone else to sell, creating a prototype of the app is always a great idea—and that's exactly what you will be doing in this first book in our *iOS App Development for Non-Programmers* series.

To be specific, you will build an app that a delivery person can use to deliver Apple products (iPhones, iPads, etc.) to customers in a metropolitan area.

You will even include a map that shows the driver's current location (maps are always fun).

You will be amazed at how much you can do without writing any code (although you *will* learn how to write code in the next book in this series).

What is a Prototype?

I like the following definition of prototype, which fits pretty closely to how the term is used throughout this book:

One of the first units manufactured of a product, which is tested so that the design can be changed if necessary before the product is manufactured commercially

Creating a Prototype is a Best Practice

This definition provides the primary motivation for creating a prototype. When you first put fingers to keyboard, you may have a rough idea of how your app will look and function when it's finished, but you will find it can and often does change drastically from its original inception.

Rather than wasting time finessing a design that is going to change, it's best to get a basic, roughly functioning version of the app into the hands of people who represent your target audience (gamers for games, teachers for educational apps, and so on). These users can provide valuable feedback that can substantially change your design. Typically, iOS apps do not come with documentation, so you need to make your app easy and intuitive to use. If you are building an app for someone else, they can show off the prototype to their customers and begin generating excitement and "buy in" for the app early on.

It's best to get this feedback as early as possible, because once you invest many hours writing code associated with a particular user-interface design, it's human nature to resist changing the design. You will find yourself far more open to valuable feedback when you have built a functioning prototype. Apple's Xcode app development tool allows you to lay out the basic user interface design and structure of your app while writing little or no code.

Building a prototype app *is* a best practice, and this book series is very much about promoting best practices in building iOS apps for the iPhone, iPad and iPod Touch.

All of This Applies to "Real" Apps

As you will find, the skills you learn in this book are directly applicable to real, fully functioning apps. The techniques for designing the user interface, laying out app navigation and designing lists of data are *exactly* the same for prototype apps and "real" apps.

Turning Pinocchio Into a Real Boy

Once your prototype app has been proved to have a solid design that works well for your target audience, it's time to turn the prototype into a "real" app. What's great about Xcode is that you don't lose the work you put into the prototype. You can keep the user-interface layout, navigation, and basic functionality of the prototype app and make changes to it to convert it to a fully-functioning app.

Before you can create a real app, you need to learn Objective-C; the programming language used to create iOS apps which is covered in the next book in this series, *iOS Apps for Non-Programmers - Book 2: Flying With Objective-C.*

You Can Do This!

In the process of reading this book and following the step-by-step instructions for creating a prototype app, you will get a taste of the app development process and build confidence that you really can build iOS apps. Half the battle is giving yourself permission to succeed and overcoming mental roadblocks for beginning the process. So let's get started!

Big Beach, Maui

Chapter 1: Getting Started

Welcome! This is the part of the book where you learn how to get yourself and your computer set for app development and discover how to get your hands on the code samples that come with this book.

Sections in This Chapter

The Cost of Becoming an Apple Developer

These days, cost is a real consideration in any new venture. Fortunately, getting into *iOS* app development isn't going to break the bank, but there are definitely some costs involved.

First of all, you need a computer on which you can create iOS apps (see the next section for details). If you already have the right computer, you have bypassed the greatest expense. Even if you don't, you can buy a brand new Mac mini for around $575.

Becoming a registered Apple Developer is free, but if you want to test your apps on an actual device (you do) and submit them to the App Store, you need to pay an annual developer fee starting at $99—but you can wait to pay this fee until you have climbed the iOS app development learning curve.

The phrase "it takes money to make money" is very true in this case. There is a great potential for getting a return on your investment as you sell apps in the App Store, or even write apps for others. This initial investment is well worth it.

Getting the Right Computer

Your first step in creating iOS apps is to get a computer on which you can run Apple's Xcode development tool.

The Right Processor

You need an Intel-based Mac to run Xcode (Macs have either a PowerPC or Intel **processor**). Any Mac built after August 2006 has an Intel processor. If you're not sure which processor your Mac has, follow these steps:

1. Click the Apple icon in the main menu on your desktop and select **About This Mac** (Figure 1.1).

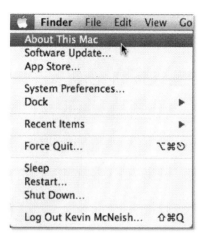

*Figure 1.1 Select **About This Mac**.*

2. In the About This Mac dialog box, look next to Processor to see which processor your Mac has (Figure 1.2).

Figure 1.2 You need a Mac with an Intel processor.

The Right Operating System

You need to make sure you have the right operating system for running Xcode. Mac computers run the OS X operating system. Apple names its operating systems after animals, along with an associated version number. The last three major operating systems released by Apple (from newest to oldest) are:

• OS X Mountain Lion (version 10.8)

• OS X Lion (version 10.7)

• OS X Snow Leopard (version 10.6)

Between major releases, Apple releases minor versions of OS X. The latest version of Xcode (version 5) runs on OS X Mountain Lion version 10.8.4 or higher. If you have an older version of OS X, you must upgrade to at least version 10.8.4.

Buying the Right Computer

If you don't already own an Intel-based Mac, the least expensive Mac you can purchase is the Mac mini. The Mac mini isn't a laptop computer, but it's a very small (7.7 x 1.4 x 7.7 inches) and lightweight (2.7 pounds) device to which you can connect your existing PC or Mac keyboard and external monitor.

You can get a Mac mini at a great price from Apple. Make sure you get the newest 2.5 GHz Mac mini model. This model comes with 4 GB of memory and a 500 GB hard drive. The processor speed (2.5 GHz) and the amount of memory (4 GB) dictate how fast your Mac mini runs. Higher processor speeds and larger memory increase your speed. The size of the hard drive (500 GB) indicates how much information you can store on your Mac mini.

If you've got a little more money to spend, I recommend the MacBook Pro. It's a powerful notebook computer that allows you to work anywhere. If you prefer a desktop computer, the iMac is a great choice with displays that range from 21.5-inch to 27-inch.

The Right Amount of Memory

How much memory do you need on your Mac? The bare minimum is 2 GB, but you should really get as much as you can afford. 4 GB of memory is much better but, if you plan to do a lot of app development, definitely invest in 8 GB. With 8 GB you won't spend time sitting on your hands waiting for Xcode to finish a task!

Downloading the Sample Code

We have created a sample project for each chapter (starting with chapter 3) that shows the completed prototype up to that point in the book. Follow these steps to download this book's sample code on your Mac (you can't download the code on an a Kindle device):

1. In the browser on your Mac, go to this link:

    http://www.iOSAppsForNonProgrammers.com/SamplesPRO.html

2. When you get to the download page, click the **Download Sample Code** link

(Figure 1.3).

Sample Code

Click this link to download the sample code for this book:

Download Sample Code

Figure 1.3 Click the Download Sample Code link.

3. If Safari is your default web browser, when you click the link, you will see a blue progress indicator in the upper right corner of the browser (Figure 1.4).

Figure 1.4 The download progress indicator

4. When the blue progress bar completely fills, and then disappears, the download is complete. To view the downloaded file, click the Show downloads button in the upper right corner of Safari (Figure 1.5).

Figure 1.5 Click the Show downloads button.

5. This displays the Downloads popup. Click the small magnifying glass on the right (Figure 1.6).

Figure 1.6 Click the magnifying glass to see the samples.

This displays the downloaded **SamplesPRO** folder in Finder (Figure 1.7).

Figure 1.7 The newly downloaded samples

6. Let's make a copy of this folder and save it the **Documents** folder (you can choose a different destination folder if you prefer).

7. With the **SamplesPRO** folder still selected, press the **Command** key (the key to the left of the spacebar), and while holding the key down, press the **C** key (in other words, press **Command+C**). This makes a copy of the folder in memory.

8. Next, on the left side of the Finder window, click the **Documents** folder as shown in Figure 1.8, and then press the **Command+V** keys to add a copy of the **SamplesPRO** folder into the **Documents** folder.

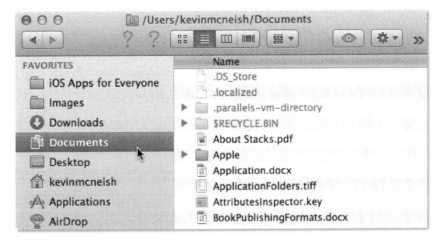

*Figure 1.8 Select the **Documents** folder.*

9. Double-click the **SamplesPRO** folder in the right-hand panel of the Finder window and you will see the sample project folders shown in Figure 1.9.

10. Now your computer is completely   set up to begin prototyping iOS apps!

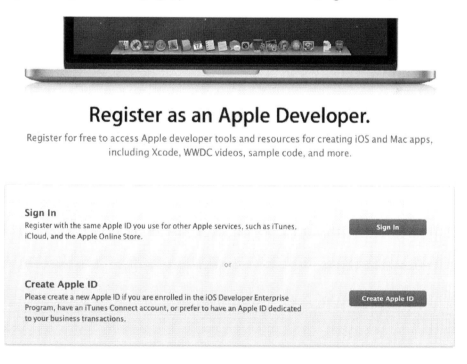

Figure 1.9 The sample project folders

Registering as an Apple Developer (free)

It's not until you register as an Apple Developer (free of charge) that you get access to all the goodness that is Apple's full iOS developer tools, documentation, and support forums. Here's where you get started:

http://developer.apple.com/programs/register/

When you navigate to this page, you have two choices (Figure 1.10).

Register as an Apple Developer.

Register for free to access Apple developer tools and resources for creating iOS and Mac apps, including Xcode, WWDC videos, sample code, and more.

Sign In
Register with the same Apple ID you use for other Apple services, such as iTunes, iCloud, and the Apple Online Store.

Sign In

or

Create Apple ID
Please create a new Apple ID if you are enrolled in the iOS Developer Enterprise Program, have an iTunes Connect account, or prefer to have an Apple ID dedicated to your business transactions.

Create Apple ID

Figure 1.10 Registering as an Apple Developer

1. **Sign In** - Choose this option to register as an Apple Developer using an existing Apple ID. You already have an Apple ID if you have an iTunes or iCloud account, or use the Apple Online Store.

2. **Create Apple ID** - If you don't have an Apple ID, or if you don't want to use your personal ID for your app development, you can create a new Apple ID.

Depending on which option you choose, you will be asked to answer various questions, and read and sign the Apple Developer Agreement.

Joining the iOS Developer Program

At some point in the process, you will be taken to a web page that talks about the different developer programs.

To get full access to the complete iOS developer experience, including the ability to take the training wheels off your apps, run them on a real iOS device, and distribute them to the App Store, you need to pay your fee (starting at $99) to become part of the iOS Developer Program.

For this book, *you only need to be registered (for free) as an Apple Developer* (you may have to scroll to the bottom of the web page to see this choice). Since there is an annual developer fee, you can choose to join an Apple Developer Program at a later date once you're past the initial iOS learning curve.

Downloading and Installing Xcode

The installation file for Xcode is huge (although it can vary between versions, it will be at least 1.4 GB).

> **Warning:** Before installing Xcode, make sure you have plenty of disk space available (at least a few gigabytes). If you don't have enough disk space available, the Xcode installer doesn't always warn you and simply displays a vague error message!

Depending on the speed of your Internet connection, plan for a relatively long download time. Once you have downloaded the installation file, it takes only 5-10 minutes to perform the actual installation.

You can download Xcode to your Mac from the App Store free of charge. To do this:

1. First click on the App Store icon (Figure 1.11).

Figure 1.11 Click the App Store icon.

If you don't see the App Store icon in your Mac's dock (usually at the bottom of the screen), try clicking the folder in the dock with the large **A** on it to bring up the Applications installed on your Mac. If all else fails, you can launch Finder and click **Applications** in the side bar. You can then select **App Store** from the list.

2. When the App Store window appears, in the upper right corner, type **Xcode** in the search box and press **Enter**. You should see **Xcode** appear in the list of results as shown in Figure 1.12.

Figure 1.12 Search for Xcode in the App Store.

3. Click on the Xcode icon and the App Store window will display details about Xcode. If this is the first time you have installed Xcode, the button below the Xcode icon will say **Free**, or, if you have a previous version of Xcode installed, the button will say **Update** as shown in Figure 1.13.

Figure 1.13 Xcode in the App Store

4. In either case, click this button and the text of the button will change to **INSTALL APP**. Click the button again, and you will be prompted for your Apple ID. After entering your Apple ID and Password, click **Sign In** and the button in the App Store window changes to say "Installing".

5. While Xcode is installing, you can do other tasks on your Mac. If you want to check the installation progress, click the **Purchases** icon at the top of the App Store window and you can check the amount of megabytes downloaded and time remaining as shown in Figure 1.14.

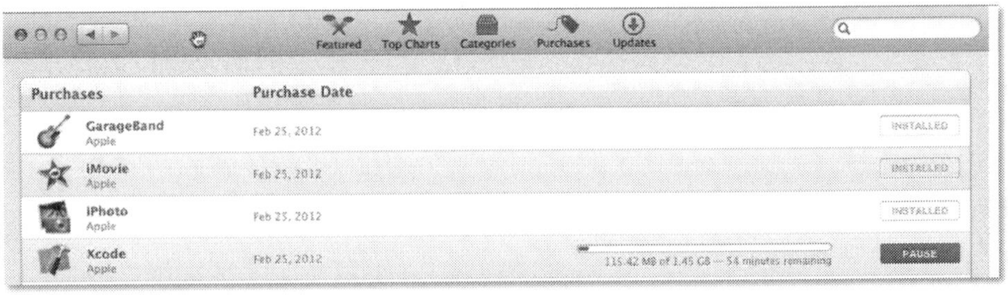

Figure 1.14 Checking Xcode's installation progress

When installation completes, if you are still on the main App Store panel, the button text changes to **Installed**.

On the App Store's **Purchases** tab, the **Xcode** item also shows it is installed (Figure 1.15).

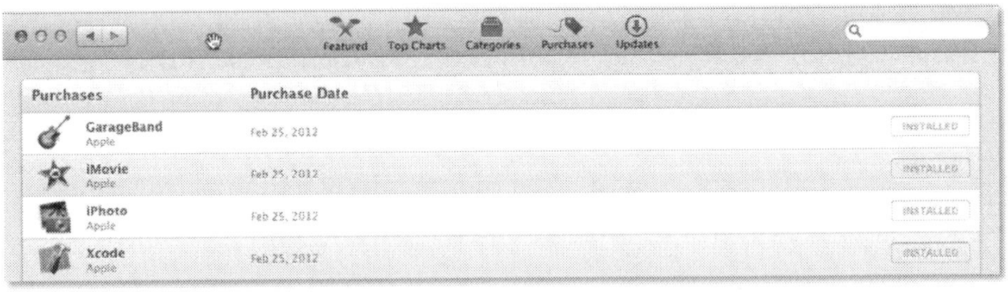

Figure 1.15 Xcode is "Installed" on the Purchases tab.

If Xcode doesn't open automatically after installation, click the **Applications** folder in your Mac OS X Dock, and then click the Xcode.app icon from the popup list of applications shown in Figure 1.16 (you may need to scroll down to see it).

Figure 1.16 Select the Xcode.app icon to launch Xcode.

6. The first time you launch Xcode, you may see an Xcode Component Installation dialog that tells you to install an additional framework or component (Figure 1.17). If you see this dialog, click **Install**, and enter the ID and Password for your computer. This installation takes just a few minutes.

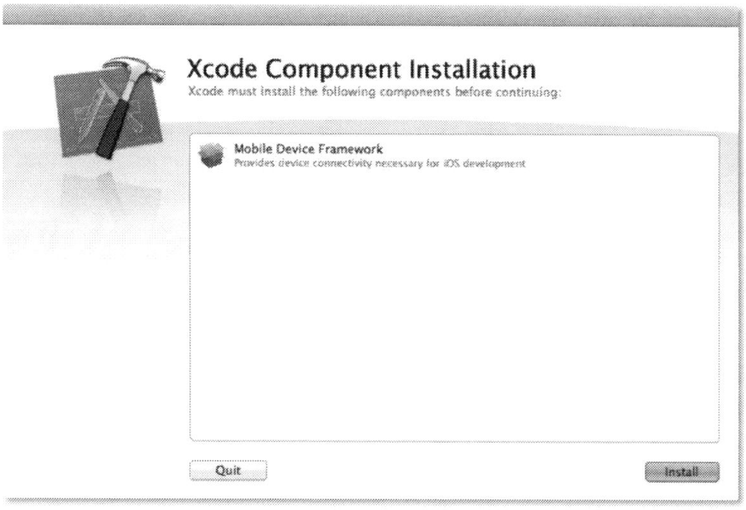

Xcode Component Installation
Xcode must install the following components before continuing:

Mobile Device Framework
Provides device connectivity necessary for iOS development

Quit   Install

Figure 1.17 Installing frameworks and components

7. When the Mobile Device Framework installation has finished, the **Installation Complete** message appears (Figure 1.18). Click **Start Using Xcode** to continue.

Figure 1.18 Installation is complete!

8. You should now see the "Welcome to Xcode" screen shown in Figure 1.19.

Figure 1.19 Xcode is installed and ready for you!

Ready to Roll!

Now that you have a Mac computer with Xcode installed, joined the iOS Developer Program and downloaded the code samples for this book, you're completely set up for iOS app development!

The next chapter introduces basic concepts important for you to understand before you begin creating your prototype. After that, you get to dive in and begin the fun of app development.

Chapter 2: Understanding the Basics

This chapter helps you understand the basics by answering questions such as "What is an app?" and "What is iOS?" The last section in this chapter contains important information about Xcode that you do *not* want to miss!

Sections in This Chapter

1. *What is an App?*

2. *Three Parts of an App*

3. *What is iOS?*

4. *Important Information About Xcode*

5. *The Cocoa Touch Framework*

6. *Summary*

What is an App?

Before diving into creating a prototype, it's best to get some context for what you will learn in upcoming chapters. A great place to start is understanding the meaning of the word *app*.

An **app** is a relatively small software *application* designed to perform one or more related tasks. In the context of this book, an app is specifically a software application that runs on an iPhone, iPod Touch or iPad.

There are two main categories of apps. First, there are built-in apps created by Apple and pre-installed on your iOS device. For example, Figure 2.1 shows four pre-installed apps—the **Contacts**, **Game Center**, **Newsstand**, and **Settings** iOS apps.

Figure 2.1 Some of the apps preinstalled on your iOS device

The second category of apps is custom apps that you have either downloaded and installed from the App Store or created yourself and loaded onto your device. Apple's Xcode lets you design and build your own custom apps.

Three Parts of an App

Before you begin creating apps, you should have a solid understanding of these main parts in order to create a well-designed application that is easy to maintain.

Here are the three main parts of an app:

- *User Interface* - This is the part of the app that the user sees and interacts with by touch. It includes buttons, text fields, lists, and, as is the case with many games, the entire touch screen surface. Also known as the *UI*.

- *Core Logic* – This is the code required to perform actions when a user-interface object is touched or any other processing takes place automatically. Whenever an app "does something," it requires code to execute a set of instructions.

- ***Data*** – The information and preferences maintained by an app. This can be as simple as storing the user's zip code or as complex as storing large amounts of data such as thousands of pictures and songs.

To get a clear understanding of these three parts of an app, let's take a close look at Apple's built-in iOS Weather app. When you first bring up the app, it displays the six-day forecast for the default city as shown in Figure 2.2.

Figure 2.2 The Weather app

- In this screen, the displays of the city, the current temperature, and the six-day forecast, including weather images and the fonts and colors used are all part of the **user interface**.

- The part of the app that goes out to the web and gets the current temperature & forecast is the **core logic**.

- The part of the app that stores the list of commonly used cities, the default city, and the temperature scale (Fahrenheit or Celsius) as well as other settings is the app's **data**.

Let's look at another screen in the same app. Tap the Yahoo! Icon in the lower left corner to go to a Yahoo! Search web page that displays weather, news, and current events (Figure 2.3).

Figure 2.3 Yahoo! Weather page

- In this screen, displays of the search box, advertisement, and the fonts and images used are part of the **user interface**.

- The part of the app that performs a web search, goes out to the Internet to get the ad text, and retrieves weather and local news is the app's **core logic**.

- The part of the app that knows the currently selected city is the app's **data**.

Let's look at one more screen in the Weather app. To get back to the built-in Weather app, just double-tap your iPhone home button and tap the Weather app icon in the list that appears at the bottom of the screen. When you're back in the app, tapping the list in the bottom-right corner leads to a list of cities for which you have selected to track weather (Figure 2.4).

Figure 2.4 The Weather app's city list

- In this screen, the display of the list of cities including their fonts, colors and images—as well as the plus (+), **Done**, **Local Weather** and Fahrenheit/Celsius buttons—are all part of the **user interface**.

- The part of the app that reads the list of cities of interest from the local device, adds new cities, and converts from Fahrenheit to Celsius is the app's **core logic**.

- The part of the app that stores the cities and the order in which they are listed is the app's **data**.

So how do you create an app's user interface, core logic, and data? The answer is *Xcode*. Apple's Xcode software allows you to lay out the user interface by means of its Interface Builder.

Xcode lets you create core logic by providing tools to write code in the Objective-C language in order to perform a wide variety of tasks. It also provides tools for designing, storing and retrieving your app's data.

What is iOS?

apps are not the only software running on an iPhone, iPod Touch or iPad. They also run an *operating system* called *iOS*, which manages the device hardware and provides the core functionality for all apps running on the device.

When you first turn on an iPhone, the Apple icon displayed on a black screen greets you. During this startup phase, the operating system gets the iPhone ready to be used. It displays the user's wallpaper and app icons. It also tries to find a carrier signal for the cell phone and a wireless signal for Wi-Fi access.

As Apple releases new versions of the iOS operating system, it continues to improve the core functionality of the device by adding new features, fixing bugs, and even releasing new built-in apps. With each release of iOS, you can add new functionality to the apps you create by taking advantage of the new features that it provides.

The type of app that you create is limited only by your imagination. You can use specific hardware and software features of iOS devices for widely different purposes. For example, you can use the microphone to record voice memos or to act as an input for a musical wind instrument (check out the *Ocarina* app for an example of this). You can use the camera not only to take pictures, but also to view details of the world around you in augmented reality apps such as the *Yelp* app. You can use Internet access to get the latest weather forecast or to retrieve a list of current political candidates. You can use the GPS to show the user's current location on a map or as an altimeter to show his or her current elevation.

Each time that you install an app on your smart phone, it gets smarter. The newly installed app empowers your phone with a new set of functionality. Now with *Siri*, the voice-activated assistant introduced in the iPhone 4s, your phone seems even smarter with a personality to go along with its intelligence (unfortunately, there is currently no way to access Siri's functionality from the apps that you create).

Important Information About Xcode

Xcode is Apple's free software development tool. You can use it to create iOS apps or Mac desktop apps (we only discuss iOS apps in this book series).

In Xcode, you can design your app's user interface, write code in the Objective-C programming language, and test your app in the iPhone and iPad Simulators.

Xcode—the Big Picture

The Xcode window is divided into five main areas as shown in Figure 2.5.

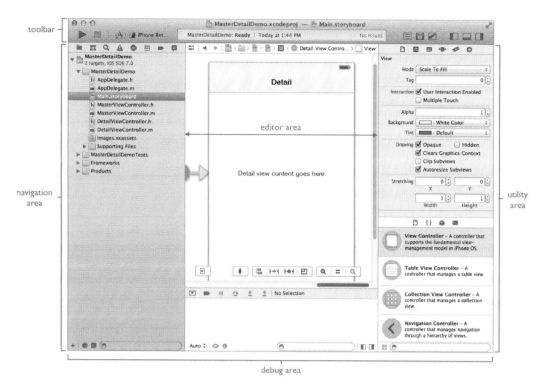

Figure 2.5 The Xcode window

- The **toolbar** at the top of the window lets you run your project in the Simulator or on a device. In the center of the toolbar, the Activity Viewer keeps you posted on the progress of tasks that Xcode performs. The toolbar buttons on the right allow you to toggle the display of editors, views and the Xcode Organizer window.

- The **navigator area** on the left contains seven navigation tools that allow you to navigate your project files, symbols, search results, issues, breakpoints, and more. The seven icons at the top of the navigation area allow you to select the different navigation tools.

- The **editor area** in the center of the window is one of the most important areas in Xcode. It's where you spend the majority of your time, whether it's designing your user interface or writing code. It's the only area in Xcode that can't be hidden. This area is home to the Interface Builder editor, code editor, and project editor.

- The **debug area** on the center bottom contains tools that help you debug your apps and contains the Variables view and the Console.

- The **utility area** on the right contains the Inspector pane (on top) including six different inspector tools that help you to create your user interface and to provide quick help when you need it. The six icons at the top of the utility area allow you to select the different inspector tools. The utility area also contains the library pane, which includes four separate libraries of UI objects, code snippets, media, and file templates. The four icons at the top of the library pane allow you to select the different libraries.

Xcode's Attributes Inspector

The tool you will be using the most in this book is Xcode's Attributes Inspector.

The Attributes Inspector (Figure 2.6) is available when you select a UI object in the Xcode design surface. You can view the Attributes Inspector by clicking the third button from the right in the Inspector toolbar.

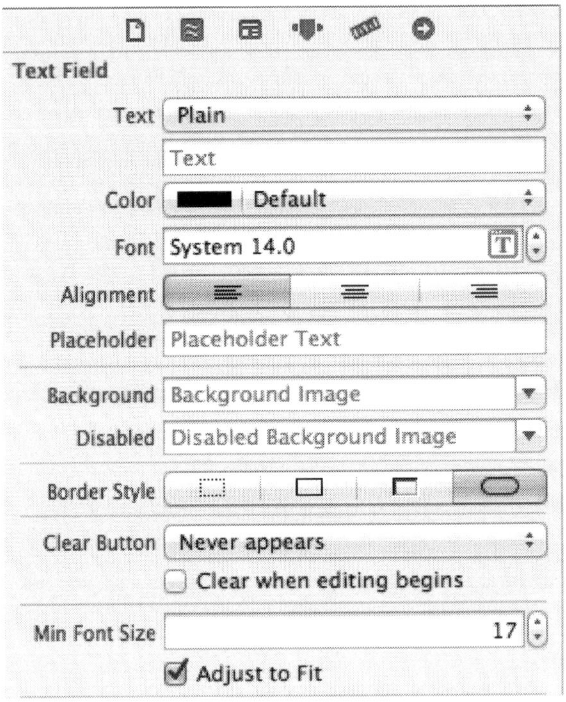

Figure 2.6 Xcode's Attributes Inspector

As you will see, user-interface objects have **attributes** that describe its characteristics—such as height, width, and color. The Attributes Inspector allows you to easily change these attributes.

Learning More About Xcode

This book contains just enough information about Xcode to allow you to create the prototype app. However, you need to get to know Xcode even better to take advantage of its full power and create the best apps possible.

To get this knowledge quickly, and learn how to create some great sample apps in the process, I recommend that you check out our third book in this series, *iOS Apps for Non-Programmers: Book 3 - Navigating Xcode*. Not only will you learn a lot about Xcode, you will also learn much about creating iOS apps as you follow step-by-step instructions in each chapter.

The Cocoa Touch Framework

Everything that you do in your app—such as designing the ***user interface*** (UI), writing the ***core logic***, and saving and retrieving ***data***—gets its functionality from Apple's ***Cocoa Touch Framework***. The Cocoa Touch Framework provides access to important services that allow your app to do great things. Cocoa Touch is actually a set of many smaller frameworks (reusable sets of tools), each focusing on a set of core functionality.

You will learn much more about the Cocoa Touch Framework later in this series—I just wanted you to understand what this term means when you come across it later on in this book!

Summary

- An *app* is a relatively small software *app*lication designed to perform one or more related tasks. In the context of this book, an app is more specifically a software application that runs on an iPhone, iPod Touch or iPad.

- There are two main categories of apps. First, there are built-in apps created by Apple and pre-installed on your iOS device. The second category of apps is custom apps, which you have either downloaded and installed from the app Store or created yourself and loaded onto your device.

- Here are the three main parts of an app:

  1. ***User Interface*** - The part of the app that the user sees and interacts with by touch. It includes buttons, text fields, lists, and, as is the case with many games, the entire touch screen surface. Also known as the ***UI***.

  2. ***Core Logic*** – This is the code required to perform actions when a user-interface object is touched or any other processing takes place automatically.

3. **Data** – The information and preferences maintained by an app.

- On an iOS device, iOS is the *operating system*. It is the software provided by Apple that manages the device hardware and provides the core functionality for all apps running on the device.

- *Xcode* is Apple's free software development tool. You can use it to create iOS apps or Mac desktop apps.

- User-interface objects have *attributes* that describe its characteristics—such as height, width, and color.

- Xcode's Attributes Inspector allows you to easily change the attributes of a user-interface object. It's the tool you will be using most often in this book.

- The *Cocoa Touch Framework* provides access to important services that allow your app to do great things. Cocoa Touch is actually a set of many smaller frameworks (reusable sets of tools), each focusing on a set of core functionality.

Chapter 3: Diving In—Creating the Project

In this chapter you will follow step-by-step instructions that show you how to create your first project in Xcode. Along the way you will learn about project templates and Xcode's Project Navigator for managing files in your project.

Sections in This Chapter

1. *A Preview of the Final Prototype App*

2. *Creating the Prototype Project*

3. *Examining the New Project*

4. *Summary*

5. *Step-By-Step Movie 3.1*

A Preview of the Final Prototype App

Before you get started, it's best to get a mental picture of what the final prototype app looks like. The prototype app is designed to be used by a person in a delivery truck to help them deliver shipments of Apple products.

This is a great app to prototype because there are many businesses that are looking for someone to create a similar delivery app for them. When the app first displays, it shows a list of **Deliveries** to be made (Figure 3.1).

Figure 3.1 A list of deliveries to be made

If you select the first delivery in the list, you are taken to the **Shipment** screen shown in Figure 3.2. This screen displays the name, address, phone, and text of the customer, as well as the delivery status, shipment ID, and the items included in the shipment.

‹ Deliveries **Shipment**

Feng Wong

3251 20th Avenue
San Francisco, CA 94132   ›

Phone (555) 392-0201

Text (555) 392-0201

Delivery Status   On Vehicle for Delivery ›

ID **1X4-56BR9-88721**

(1) iPod Touch

(1) Apple TV

Figure 3.2 Shipment details

If the user taps the address (the second item in the list) in the **Shipment** screen, it takes you to the Location screen shown in Figure 3.3.

Figure 3.3 The map shows the delivery location.

The map shows the delivery location, but the map is not zoomed in yet. At the bottom-right corner is an info button. When the user taps this button, the Map Options scene is displayed as shown in Figure 3.4.

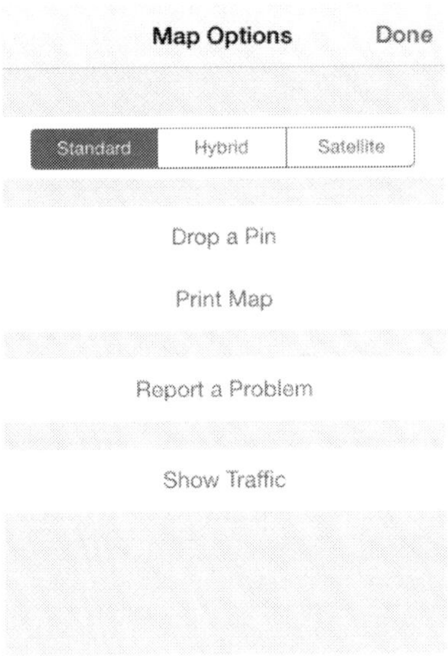

Figure 3.4 The Map Options scene

If the user taps the **Delivery Status** item in the **Shipment** screen, it takes them to the **Delivery Status** screen (Figure 3.5). In the prototype, the first item is always selected. Later in this book series we'll add some code that allows the user to change the delivery status.

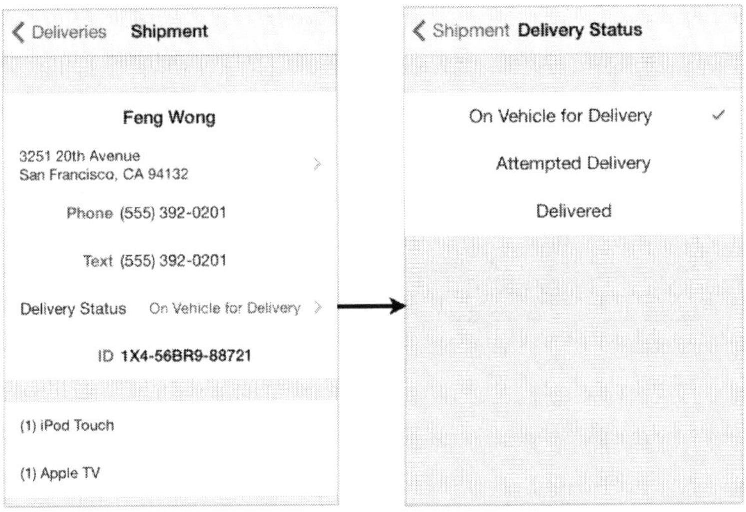

*Figure 3.5 Navigating to the **Delivery Status** screen*

The check mark next to **On Vehicle for Delivery** in the screen on the right indicates that this is the current status of the delivery. This matches the blue text in the **Delivery Status** item in the **Shipment** screen on the left.

As you shall see when you follow the step-by-step instructions, you can create this prototype without writing a single line of code. Let's get started.

Creating the Prototype Project

Follow the steps in this section to create the new prototype project.

1. If it's not already open, launch Xcode.

2. If you have another project open in Xcode, close it by selecting **File > Close Project** from the Xcode menu. You can also just click the red button in the upper left corner of the Xcode window.

   You can work in multiple projects at the same time in Xcode, but for new programmers it's easier to just have one project open at a time.

3. If the Welcome to Xcode window is displayed, select the option to **Create a new Xcode project** on the left side of the dialog. Otherwise, from the Xcode menu, select the **File > New > Project...** option (Figure 3.6).

Figure 3.6 The menu option to create a new project

In either case, this displays the New Project dialog shown in Figure 3.7.

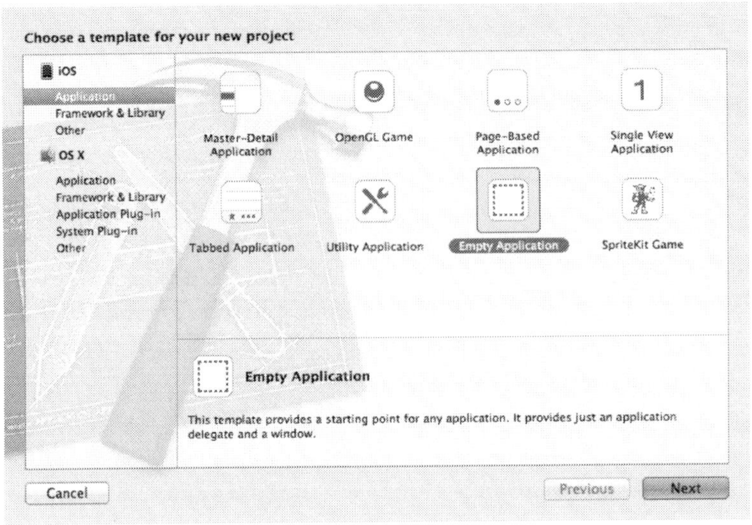

*Figure 3.7 Select the **Empty Application** template.*

Since you can create both iOS and Mac OS X desktop applications using Xcode, the panel on the left side of the dialog has options for both types of applications. However, because you are creating iOS apps, you should always select one of the sub-items under **iOS** when creating a new project.

4. Under the **iOS** templates section, select **Application**. This displays a list of associated project templates on the right. Each template gives you a slightly different starting project that gives you a head start in the right direction for the specific type of app that you intend to create. Ultimately, after you create your project, you can change it to be just like any one of the other project templates.

5. On the right side of the dialog, select the **Empty Application** project template as shown in Figure 3.7.

    This project template is a good choice for a prototype app because other templates add unnecessary code to the project that you have to remove. It's also educational to learn how to create a project from scratch!

6. Click the **Next** button. This displays the next step of the New Project dialog as shown in Figure 3.8.

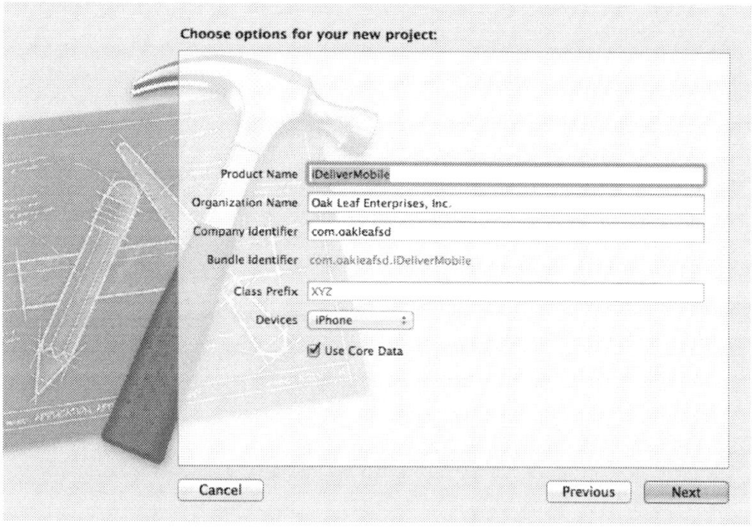

Figure 3.8 Second step of the new project dialog

7. In the **Product Name** box, enter **iDeliverMobile**. This specifies the name of your app and the name of the project. Although you can enter spaces in the product name, I prefer not to because Xcode also names some of the classes based on the product name and converts any spaces to underscores (_), which gets ugly.

8. In the **Organization Name** box, enter the name of your company, or just your name if you don't have a company.

9. The **Company Identifier** is part of the information used to uniquely identify your product. A great way to make this identifier unique is to use a web address in the format **com.yourcompany**. For example, my company identifier is **com.oakleafsd**. If you don't have a company name, you can just use **edu.self**.

   After entering the product name and company identifier, notice that these two pieces of information are joined together (***concatenated*** in programming jargon) to create the ***bundle identifier*** (Figure 3.9). The bundle identifier is Apple's way of uniquely identifying your app.

Product Name	iDeliverMobile
Organization Name	Oak Leaf Enterprises, Inc.
Company Identifier	com.oakleafsd
Bundle Identifier	com.oakleafsd.iDeliverMobile

Figure 3.9 The bundle identifier is created by joining the company identifier and product name end-to-end.

10. Let's leave the **Class Prefix** empty. This option is used when you are creating new code files, but you won't be doing that in this book, so let's move on.

11. For this app, just set **Devices** to **iPhone** since we are only going to create an iPhone prototype for now. The **Devices** selection box offers three options:

   • iPad – Creates an app that only runs on the iPad
   • iPhone – Creates an app that only runs on the iPhone
   • Universal – Creates an app that runs on both the iPhone and the iPad

12. Uncheck the **Use Core Data** data option. This option is intended for apps that store data on the user's device. Even if you *do* want your app to store data on a user's device, don't select this option. The architecture of the code added to your project when this option is selected is *not* a best practice. You'll learn more about this later in this book series.

13. Click **Next**. This displays the Save dialog shown in **Figure 3.10**. Leave the **Create local git repository for this project** unchecked. This option provides version control for your project, but we don't need it for this simple sample app.

14. You can store the new project in any folder you like. As shown in Figure 3.10, I have selected the **Documents** folder on the left of the dialog.

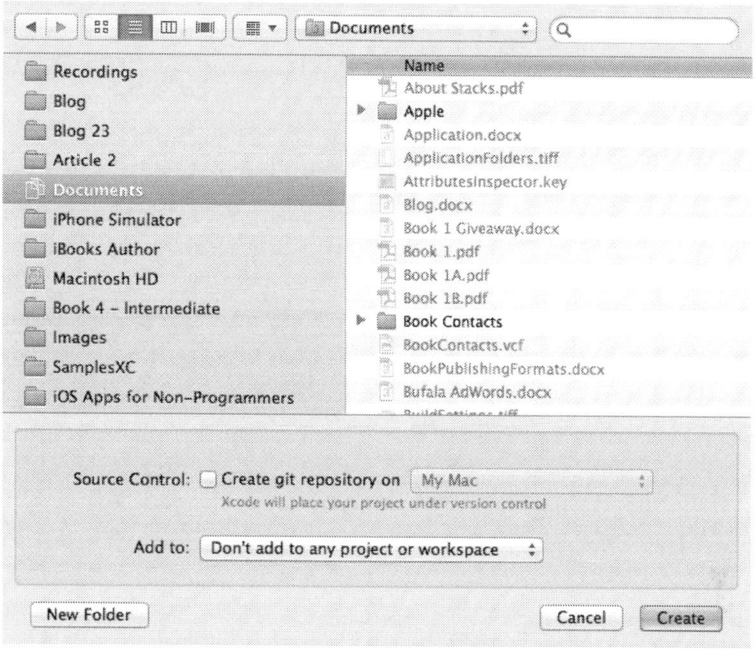

Figure 3.10 The Save dialog saves your project files.

15. Click the **Create** button to create the new project files in the directory you have selected.

Examining the New Project

When Xcode finishes creating the project, the Project Navigator pane on the left side of the Xcode window contains a list of files in the project (Figure 3.11). Since you selected the Empty Project template, the project only has a few files in it. If you are using an older version of Xcode, you may need to click the white arrow to the left of the **iDeliverMobile** node to see the files contained within it.

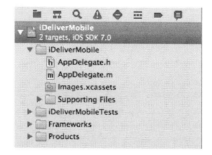

Figure 3.11 The new *iDeliverMobile* project

The folders in the Project Navigator are called *groups*. A group is a means for organizing related files together. When you create a new project, there are already several groups added to your project. However, groups do not directly correspond to folders on your Mac's hard drive! They are simply a logical grouping of related items.

You will learn more about some of these files and groups contained in the Project Navigator later on in this book.

Summary

- You can work in multiple projects at the same time in Xcode, but for new programmers it's easier to just have one project open at a time.

- You can create a new project in the Welcome to Xcode window by selecting Create a new Xcode project on the left side of the dialog. You can also create a new project from the Xcode menu by selecting the File > New > Project... option.

- In the New Project dialog, you should always select one of the sub-items under iOS when creating a new project (Figure 3.7).

- The Empty Application project template is a good choice when creating a prototype app because other templates add unnecessary code to the project that you have to remove.

- Concatenate refers to the process of joining two string together end-to-end.

- The bundle identifier is Apple's way of uniquely identifying your app. By default, it is comprised of your company identifier and product name joined together.

- The folders in the Project Navigator are called groups. A group is a means for organizing related files together.

- Groups do not directly correspond to folders on your Mac's hard drive.

Step-By-Step Movie 3.1

In case you missed any of the steps along the way, go to the following link in your web browser to see each step performed for you.

http://www.iOSAppsForNonProgrammers.com/B1M31.7.html

Chapter 4: Storyboarding & Navigation

In this chapter you are introduced to the concept of storyboards, navigation, and view controllers as you begin to lay out the beginnings of your app's user interface. You also get to see the app running in the iPhone Simulator!

Sections in This Chapter

1. *Understanding Storyboards*

2. *Adding a Storyboard to the Project*

3. *Understanding Navigation Controllers*

4. *Adding a Navigation Controller*

5. *Understanding Table Views*

6. *Understanding View Controllers*

7. *Configuring the Storyboard*

8. *Building the Project*

9. *Running the app in the Simulator*

10. *Summary*

11. *Step-By-Step Movie 4.1*

Understanding Storyboards

In this chapter you will add a ***storyboard*** to the project. A storyboard is a design surface on which you create a visual representation of your app's user interface and navigational flow in a graphical, user-friendly way.

Figure 4.1 shows how the completed storyboard for this prototype project will look when you're finished (tap the figure to zoom in for a closer look).

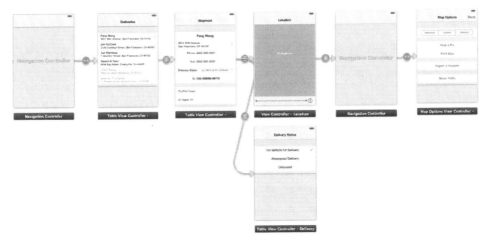

Figure 4.1 The completed storyboard

The iPhone-shaped rectangles are called ***scenes***, and they each represent one screen of information displayed to the user (you will also hear them referred to as ***views***). The lines with arrows connecting the scenes are ***segues*** which you will learn more about in the next chapter.

The storyboard allows you to lay out the scenes in your app in the order in which they are presented to the user. This makes it easy to see at a glance the basic navigational flow of your app.

Adding a Storyboard to the Project

Let's add a storyboard to the project to see how it works.

1. In Xcode, open the **iDeliverMobile** project you created in the previous chapter (you can select **File > Open Recent** from the Xcode menu and then select the **iDeliverMobile** project).

2. Select the **iDeliverMobile** group folder in the Project Navigator (Figure 4.2).

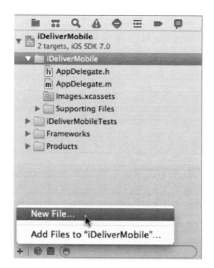

Figure 4.2 Adding a new file to the project

3. At the bottom left of the Project Navigator, click the plus (+) button in the toolbar as shown in Figure 4.2 and select **New File...** from the popup menu.

4. This displays the New File dialog. On the left side of the dialog, under the **iOS** section, select **User Interface**. On the right side of the dialog, a list of user-interface-related file templates is displayed. Select the **Storyboard** template (Figure 4.3).

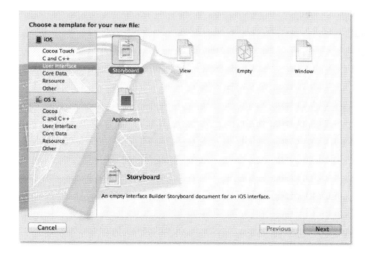

Figure 4.3 Select the Storyboard file template.

5. Click the **Next** button. In the next step of the dialog, in the **Device Family** combo box, select **iPhone** because we will make this prototype for the iPhone only (Figure 4.4).

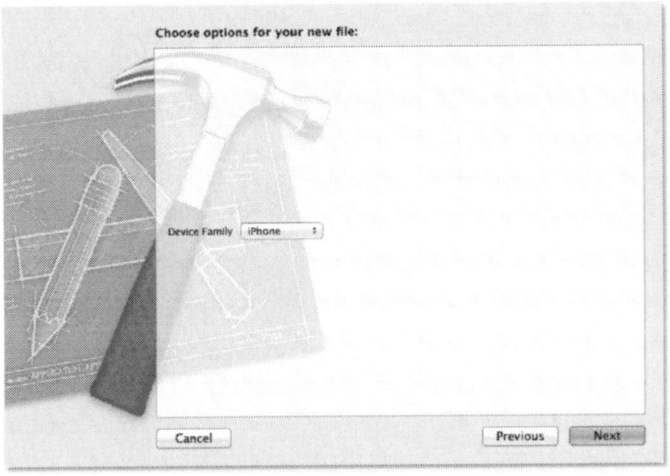

Figure 4.4 Select the iPhone Device Family.

6. Click the **Next** button. This displays the Save File dialog. By default, new files are saved in the project's root, or main folder, which is good. Just change the name of the file to **MainStoryboard.storyboard**. Afterwards, at the bottom of the dialog in the **Targets** section, select the **iDeliverMobile** checkbox (Figure 4.5) and then click the **Create** button.

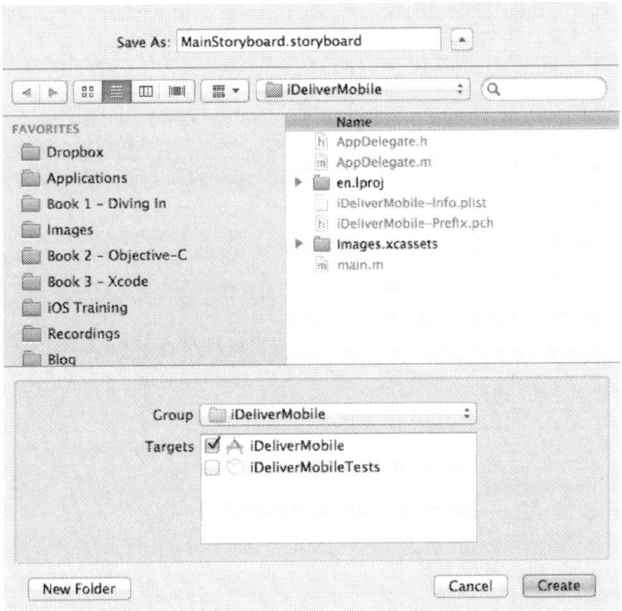

*Figure 4.5 Change the name of the file to **MainStoryboard.storyboard**.*

7. This adds the new storyboard file to the Project Navigator as shown in Figure 4.6. The storyboard file is displayed in the center area of the Xcode window, also known as the ***Interface Builder*** editor. It looks like a plain white sheet of paper.

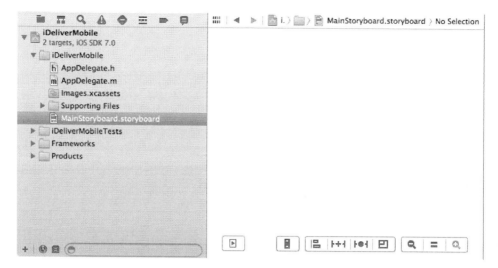

*Figure 4.6 The new **MainStoryboard.storyboard** file*

Understanding Navigation Controllers

In an iOS app, a ***navigation controller*** is responsible for managing the navigation between different scenes, or views. It presents a ***navigation bar*** at the top of the screen, (Figure 4.7) which contains a back button as well as other optional buttons you can add and customize.

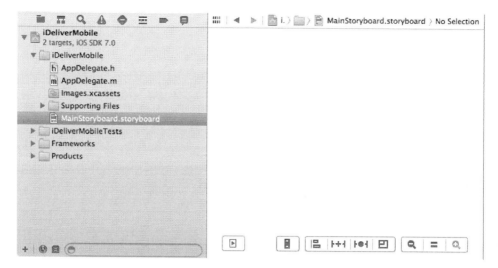

Figure 4.7 The navigation bar at the top of the screen

Adding a Navigation Controller

The navigation controller is usually the first scene in a storyboard since it controls all the other scenes. Let's add one now.

1. Make sure the **MainStoryboard.storyboard** file is selected in Xcode's Project Navigator.

2. Next, display Xcode's Object Library located in the bottom right corner of the Xcode window (Figure 4.8). If it's not visible, select **View** > **Utilities** > **Show Object Library** from the Xcode menu.

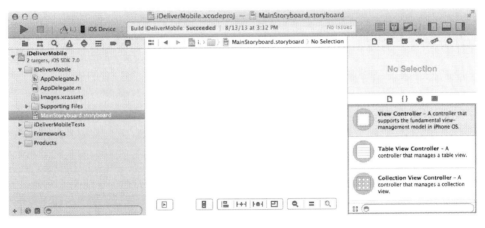

Figure 4.8 The Object Library

3. Next, drag a **Navigation Controller** from the Object Library and drop it on the storyboard (Figure 4.9).

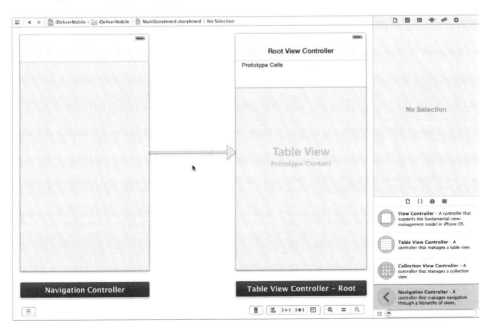

Figure 4.9 Add a navigation controller to the storyboard.

After you drop it on the storyboard, there are a few things to notice (Figure 4.10).

Figure 4.10 A navigation and root view controller

First of all, on the left side of the storyboard is an arrow pointing to the navigation controller. This indicates the navigation controller is the first scene to be displayed.

More obvious is the **Root View Controller** scene that was automatically added to the storyboard to the right of the navigation controller. This root view controller contains a table view that can contain a list of items. Xcode assumes that since you added a navigation controller, you want a list of items displayed when your app first launches (usually a good assumption).

Let's find out more about table views.

Understanding Table Views

Table views are used to display lists of data in iOS apps. If you have an iOS device of your own, you have used table views frequently, since they are found in most of Apple's built-in apps such as Settings (Figure 4.11), iTunes, Photos, Mail,

Weather, and Contacts.

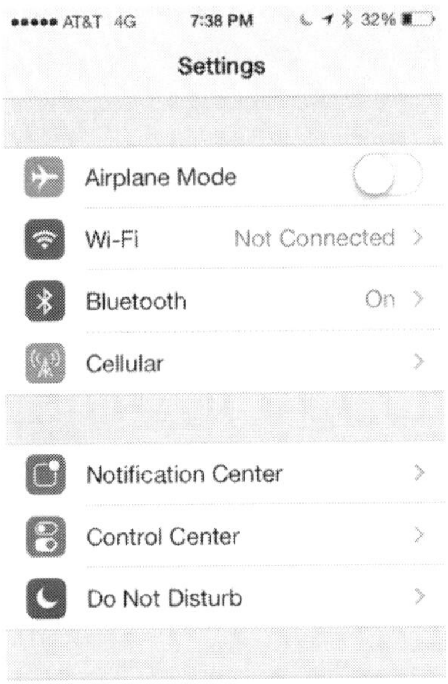

Figure 4.11 A table view in the Settings app

Each item in the table view is a **row** and a table view can contain an unlimited number of rows. Each row is one column wide and can contain an image, text, and an accessory icon, such as the **disclosure indicator** (the grey arrow) shown on the right side of the rows in Figure 4.11.

Each division of a table view is a **section**. If you have no divisions, you have only one section. For example, in Figure 4.11, the table view has two sections.

Understanding View Controllers

As you have already learned, there is a navigation root controller that controls navigation between all the scenes in your app. However, each scene, or view, also has its own **view controller**. For example, the table view that was automatically added to the storyboard has a specialized view controller known as a **table view controller** (Figure 4.12).

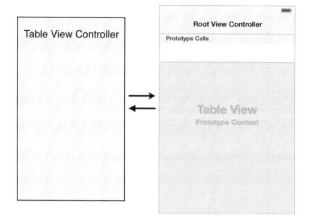

Figure 4.12 A table view controller and a table view

This table view controller works behind the scenes performing the following tasks:

- Displays the table view

- Fills the table view with data

- Responds to the user interacting with the table view

In a prototype app, the table view controller does all these things except fill the table view with data. That's because the data is manually entered into the table view at design time, as you will see in the next chapter.

Ultimately, when you are building a prototype, the fact that a view has an associated view controller is not as important as when converting the prototype to a "real" app. I just wanted to give you this background so you are not confused when adding *view controllers* to the storyboard (rather than adding *views*).

Configuring the Storyboard

Let's get back to the storyboard. When you add a storyboard to a project, as you did earlier in this chapter, you need to tell Xcode that the new storyboard is the *main* storyboard file so it gets loaded automatically when you run the app (you *can* have more than one storyboard in a project, although you normally won't).

1. To do this, in the Project Navigator, select the project node (the very first node at the top). This displays the project editor (Figure 4.13).

Figure 4.13 Selecting the project node displays the Project Editor.

2. Next, in the **Main Interface** combo box, select **MainStoryboard** as shown in Figure 4.14.

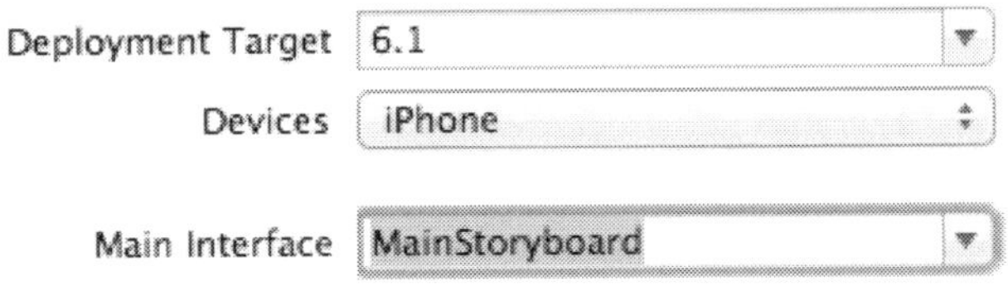

*Figure 4.14 Set **MainStoryboard** as the **Main Interface**.*

3. There's one more step you need to take to get the main storyboard to display when you run the app. In the Project Navigator, select the **AppDelegate.m** file. This file contains program code that runs when you first launch the app. Near the top of the code file is a block of code named **application: didFinishLaunchingWithOptions:** (Figure 4.15).

```
- (BOOL)application:(UIApplication *)application
    didFinishLaunchingWithOptions:(NSDictionary *)
    launchOptions
{
    self.window = [[UIWindow alloc] initWithFrame:
        [[UIScreen mainScreen] bounds]];
    // Override point for customization after
        application launch.
    self.window.backgroundColor = [UIColor
        whiteColor];
    [self.window makeKeyAndVisible];
    return YES;
}
```

Figure 4.15 Locate this code near the top of the file.

4. Select all of the code in this method except for the **return YES** statement at

the bottom of the code block. To do this, click on the far left of the first line of code, and then hold the mouse button and drag your mouse pointer down until all but the last line of code is selected.

5. Now delete the selected code by pressing the **Delete** key. When you're finished, the block of code should look like Figure 4.16.

```
- (BOOL)application:(UIApplication *)application
    didFinishLaunchingWithOptions:(NSDictionary *)
    launchOptions
{
    return YES;
}
```

Figure 4.16 The code block with code removed

Building the Project

Now you're ready to tell Xcode to *build* the project. When Xcode builds a project, it examines all the files in the project for errors and, if all is well, creates a single app file that can be run in Xcode's Simulator (which you'll see in just a bit) or on an actual iOS device.

1. To build the project, press the **Command** key (the key to the left of the spacebar), and while holding the key down, press the **B** key (in other words, press **Command+B**).

2. In the *Activity Viewer* in the top center of the Xcode window, you should see the message **Build iDeliverMobile: Succeeded** on the left, and **No Issues** on the right as shown in Figure 4.17.

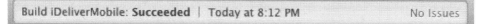
Build iDeliverMobile: Succeeded | Today at 8:12 PM   No Issues

Figure 4.17 Build succeeded, no issues

3. Before running the app in the Simulator, we are going to make one small change. In the storyboard, locate the **Root View Controller** that contains the table view, and click on the gray area labeled **Table View Prototype Content** as shown in Figure 4.18.

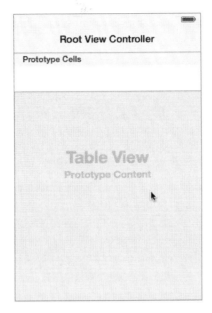

*Figure 4.18 Select the gray **Prototype Content** area.*

8. Next, go to Xcode's Attributes Inspector contained in the Utilities panel on the right side of the Xcode window as shown in Figure 4.19.

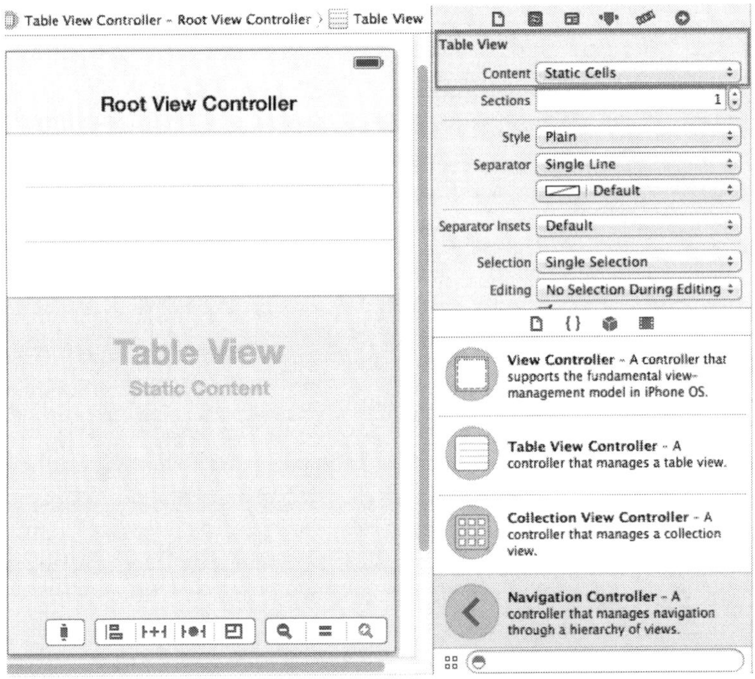

Figure 4.19 The Attributes Inspector

If the Utilites panel is not visible, select **View > Utilities > Show Utilities** in the Xcode menu. Then, to display the Attributes Inspector, select the third button from the right in the Inspector toolbar.

Before you change a setting in an Inspector, it's always a good idea to look at the very top section heading to make sure you have the correct object selected in the design surface. In this case, you should see the text **Table View** when the table view is selected (Figure 4.19).

Now change the **Content** attribute from **Dynamic Prototype** to **Static Cells**.

When you change this setting, the appearance of the table view cells changes as shown in Figure 4.19.

The *cells* that you set up at design time are used to produce *rows* in the table view at *run time* (when the app is running in the Simulator or on an iOS device). Rather than filling the cells with dynamic content at run time, you will be adding static content at design time.

Running the App in the Simulator

In the next chapter, you will customize the cells in this table view. For now, let's run the app to see how it looks.

1. First, make sure the **Scheme** setting in the toolbar at the top of the Xcode window is set to **iPhone Retina 3.5 inch** (Figure 4.20).

*Figure 4.20 Set the scheme to **iPhone Retina (3.5 inch)**.*

2. Click the **Run** button in the upper-left corner of the Xcode window (Figure 4.20) to run the app in the iPhone Simulator.

After several seconds you should see a table view displayed in the iPhone Simulator like the one shown in Figure 4.21.

Figure 4.21 The Prototype app begins to take shape!

3. If the Xcode window is visible, you can just click on it to go back to Xcode.

- Otherwise, press **Command+Tab** to go back to Xcode. When you're back in Xcode, press the **Stop** button to stop the app from running in the Simulator.

If this is your first time running an app in the iPhone Simulator, it's pretty exciting! Now that you have the structure of the first screen in place, you will set up the data in the table view in the next chapter.

Summary

- A *storyboard* is a design surface on which you create a visual representation of your app's user interface and navigation in a graphical, user-friendly way.

- The iPhone-shaped rectangles are called *scenes*, and they each represent one screen of information displayed to the user (you will also hear them referred to as *views*).

- The lines with arrows connecting the scenes are *segues*.

- A *navigation controller* is responsible for managing the navigation between different scenes, or views. It presents a navigation bar at the top of the screen which contains a back button as well as other optional buttons you can add and customize.

- *Table views* are used to display lists of data.

- Each item in the table view is a *row* and a table view can contain an unlimited number of rows.

- Each row is one column wide and can contain an image, text, and an accessory icon such as a *disclosure indicator*.

- Each division of a table view is a *section*. If you have no divisions, you have only one section.

- Every table view has an associated *table view controller*.

- The table view controller is responsible for displaying the table view at run time, filling the table view with data and responding to the user interacting with the table view.

- In a prototype app, the table view controller doesn't fill the table view with data because the data is manually entered into the table view at design time.

- In Xcode, when you add a table view controller to a storyboard, it automatically adds an associated table view too.

- When you manually add a storyboard to a project, you need to tell Xcode you want to set the new storyboard as the main storyboard file so it gets loaded automatically when you run the app.

- When Xcode *builds* a project, it examines all the files in the project for errors and, if all is well, creates a single app file that can be run in Xcode's Simulator or on an actual iOS device.

The *Activity Viewer* is an area at the top center of the Xcode window that displays status messages, project build warnings and errors, as well as the progress of tasks currently executing.

Step-By-Step Movie 4.1

In case you missed any of the steps along the way, go to the following link in your web browser to see each step performed for you.

http://www.iOSAppsForNonProgrammers.com/B1M41.7.html

Chapter 5: Displaying Lists of Data

In this chapter you will add static data to the Deliveries table view that you created in the previous chapter. You are going to change the table view style as well as the font sizes & colors of the cells to be easily read by the delivery person.

Sections in This Chapter

1. *The Interface Builder Editor*

2. *Changing the Table View Title & Style*

3. *Configuring the Table View Cells*

4. *Creating More Cells*

5. *Indicating Delivered vs. Undelivered*

6. *Toggling Retina 4 Form Factor*

7. *Running the Deliveries Scene*

8. *Summary*

9. *Step-By-Step Movie 5.1*

The Interface Builder Editor

Before making any changes to the app, let's take a necessary detour and learn more about how to work with the Interface Builder editor (Figure 5.1).

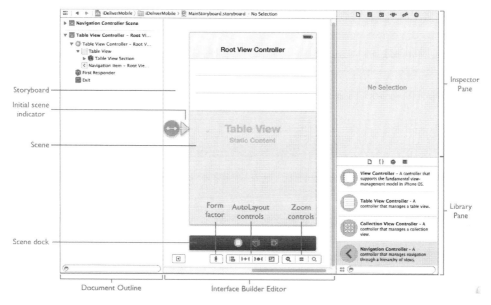

Figure 5.1 The Interface Builder editor

The Interface Builder editor is automatically opened in the main workspace window when you select a user-interface file in the Project Navigator (tap the figure to view it in full screen mode).

Scenes and Scene Docks

The Interface Builder Editor in the center pane of the Xcode window in Figure 5.1 contains a storyboard where you design your user interface. As mentioned, each iPhone screen on the storyboard is known as a *scene* or a *view*. You can add multiple scenes to the storyboard using "segues" (you will learn about these in the next chapter) that specify navigation between the scenes.

On each scene, you can drop user-interface controls from the Object Library (located in the bottom right corner of the Xcode window). Afterwards, you can use the Inspectors (upper right corner) to position, size, and set a variety of attributes to suit your needs.

The dark rectangular area below the scene is known as the ***scene dock***. It contains an icon on the left that represents the first responder (the object with which the user is currently interacting). The icon in the center represents the first responder (the object with which the user is currently interacting). The icon on the right can be used to exit the scene.

Document Outline

On the left side of Figure 5.1, the Document Outline provides a hierarchical view of all UI objects on the currently selected scene. This comes in handy when you create a more complex user interface—where one set of controls overlays another set of controls such that selecting controls directly in the view becomes difficult.

At the bottom left of the Interface Builder Editor is a gray, circular button containing a white arrow that allows you to hide and show the Document Outline. You can also show and hide the Document Outline from the Xcode menu by selecting **Editor > Show Document Outline** and **Editor > Hide Document Outline**, respectively. If the Document Outline is hidden, you can also make it visible by first selecting an object on the design surface and then selecting **Editor > Reveal in Document Outline**. This shows the Document Outline with the object selected.

Whenever you select a UI object in the Document Outline, the corresponding control in the scene gets selected, and vice-versa. You can also drag UI objects from the Object Library and drop them on the Document Outline, automatically adding them to the currently selected scene.

Now you're ready to start making some changes!

Changing the Table View Title & Style

In this section you will change both the title and style of the Deliveries scene you created in the previous chapter.

1. If it's not already open, in Xcode, open the **iDeliverMobile** project.

2. Select the **MainStoryboard.storyboard file** in the Project Navigator, and look at the scene containing the table view.

3. Double-click the title of the navigation bar labeled **Root View Controller** at the top of the scene. This puts the title into "edit mode" as shown in Figure 5.2.

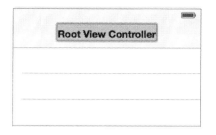

Figure 5.2 Edit the Root View Controller's title.

It's a good idea to change the title in the navigation bar first because this changes its description in the Document Outline pane.

4. Change the title of the navigation bar to **Deliveries** as shown in Figure 5.3.

*Figure 5.3 Change the navigation bar title to **Deliveries**.*

5. In the Interface Builder editor, in the Root View Controller scene, click the gray area that says **Table View Static Content**. In the Attribute Inspector, change the **Style** to **Grouped**. This changes the table view cells to take on the "grouped" look shown in Figure 5.4.

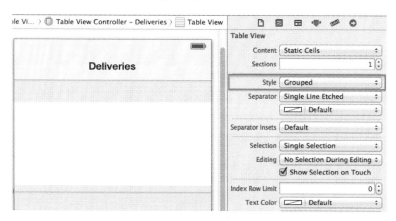

*Figure 5.4 Set the table view's **Style** to **Grouped**.*

Configuring the Table View Cells

In this section you will set up the cells in the Deliveries scene's table view. There is *much* you will learn in this section that you can use in both prototype and "real" iOS apps, so let's begin!

1. In the Document Outline pane under the **Table View Controller – Deliveries Scene**, select the **Table View Section** node (Figure 5.5). If you don't see the Document Outline pane, select the rounded-rectangle arrow button at the bottom left of the Interface Builder editor, or select **Editor > Show Document Outline** from the Xcode menu.

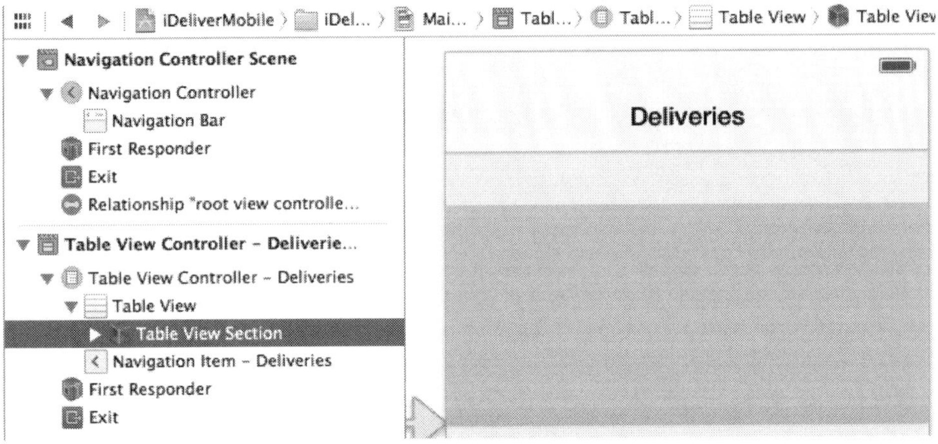

*Figure 5.5 Select **Table View Section**.*

2. In the Attributes Inspector, change the number of rows to **1** (Figure 5.6). You can either enter the number in the box, or click the down arrow twice.

Figure 5.6 Set the table view section's row count to 1.

This removes the last two cells in the table view. You are removing the other two rows because you are going to customize the style and font of one cell, then make a copy of it for the other cells in the table.

3. In the Interface Builder editor, select the one remaining table view cell. In the Attributes Inspector, set the **Style** to **Subtitle**. This displays a large **Title** and a smaller **Subtitle** beneath it (Figure 5.7).

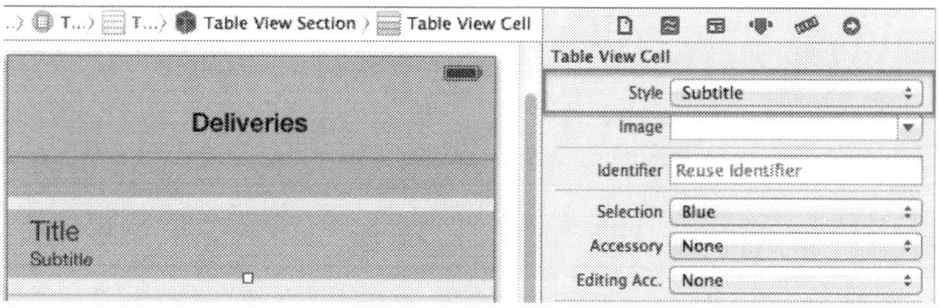

*Figure 5.7 Set the **Style** of the table view cell to **Subtitle**.*

4. Double-click the **Title** text in the table view cell. This puts the text in edit mode (Figure 5.8).

*Figure 5.8 The **Title** label in edit mode*

5. Go to the Attributes Inspector, and click the down arrow to the right of the **Font** setting to change the font size to **15** as shown in Figure 5.9.

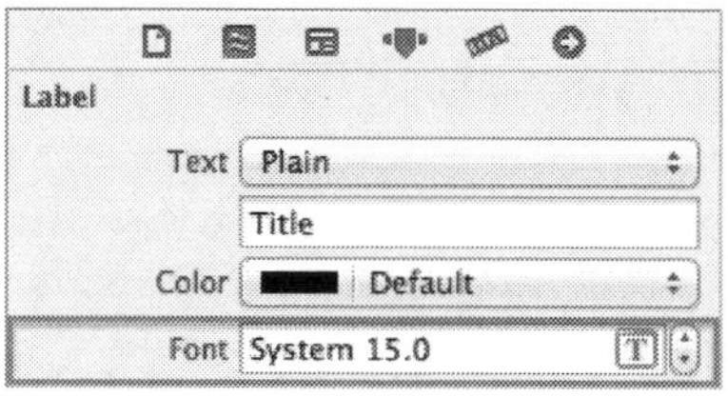

*Figure 5.9 Change the font of the **Title** text.*

To see the font setting changes take effect in the **Title** text, click anywhere in the design surface to deselect the **Title** text.

6. Now double-click the **Subtitle** text in the table view cell to put the text in edit mode. Go back to the Attributes Inspector and click the down arrow to the right of the **Font** setting to change the font size to **13**. Leave the **Subtitle** text in edit mode.

7. With the **Subtitle** text still in edit mode, go to the Attributes Inspector and in the **Autoshrink** combo box select **Minimum Font Size** (Figure 5.10).

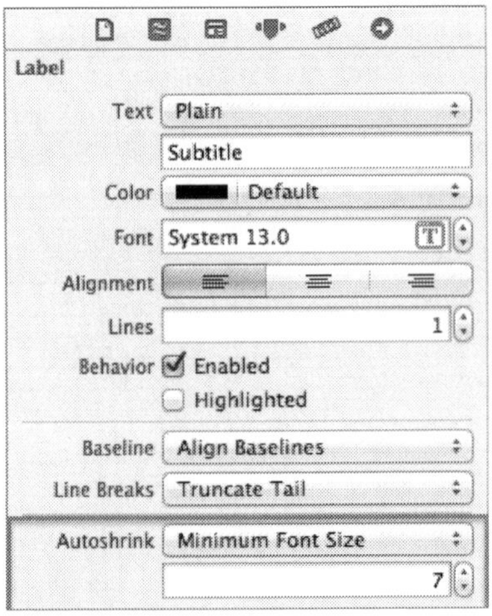

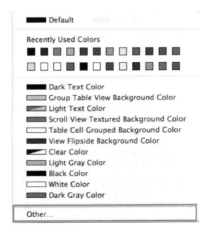

*Figure 5.10 Setting the **Autoshrink** attributes*

When this option is selected, the text in the address line (which can potentially be longer than the available space) will shrink to fit in the available space.

8. Below the combo box, leave the minimum size to 7. This indicates the smallest font size to which you want the text to shrink. If you get a really long address, an ellipsis (...) appears at the end of the line, indicating the full address doesn't fit in the available space.

9. With the **Subtitle** text still in edit mode, look a little further down in the Attributes Inspector and locate the **Text Color** attribute. Click the double-headed arrow to the right of the **Text Color** attribute to display the Color popup (Figure 5.11).

Figure 5.11 Change the font color using the Color popup.

10. At the bottom of the Color popup, select the **Other...** option. This displays

the Color Chooser. If you don't see rows of crayons, select the **Crayons** button on the far right of the Color Choose toolbar (Figure 5.12).

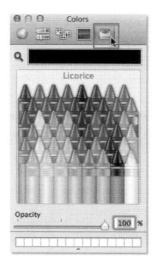

*Figure 5.12 Select the **Crayons** button.*

11. In the box of crayons, select the dark blue crayon in the middle of the top row. When you select it, you will see the name of the color is **Midnight**. Close the Color Chooser by clicking the red **X** in the upper left corner.

12. Click anywhere else in the design surface to get the **Subtitle** out of edit mode and see the effect of these changes. The **Title** and **Subtitle** text should now look like Figure 5.13.

*Figure 5.13 The updated **Title** and **Subtitle***

Creating More Cells

Now that you have set the style and fonts for the table view cell, it's time to duplicate the cell to make others just like it.

1. Select the cell by clicking on it once. Next, press **Command+D** (for "duplicate") five times to create five more cells. When you're done you should see a total of six cells that look exactly like the original cell (Figure 5.14).

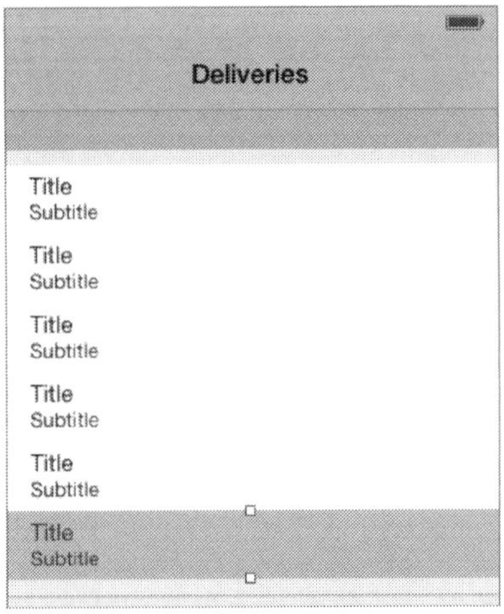

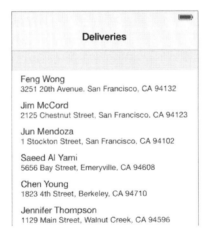

Figure 5.14 Create duplicates of the selected cell.

4. Now you can go back and edit each cell. Change the **Title** text to the name of a person and the **Subtitle** to an address (just double-click them and type the text directly in the cell). If you want ideas for names and addresses, check out Figure 5.15, where you can see fictitious names and real addresses (each address is the address of an Apple Store in the San Francisco Bay area).

*Figure 5.15 Change the **Title** and **Subtitle** of each cell.*

Indicating Delivered vs. Undelivered

In this app, if a delivery has been made, the name and address are shown in light gray. So, let's change the last few cells to look as if they have been delivered.

1. Click the last cell in the table view to select it, and then double-click the name to edit it. In the Attributes Inspector, click the double-headed arrow on the right of the **Text Color** control to display the Color popup. Select **Light Gray Color** (Figure 5.16).

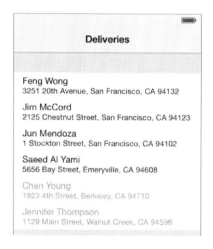

*Figure 5.16 Change the text color to **Light Gray Color**.*

2. Next, change the color of the **Subtitle** in the last cell to **Light Gray Color**.

3. Change the color of both the name and addresses in the second-to-last cell text to **Light Gray Color**. When you're done, your cells should look like Figure 5.17.

Deliveries

Feng Wong
3251 20th Avenue, San Francisco, CA 94132

Jim McCord
2125 Chestnut Street, San Francisco, CA 94123

Jun Mendoza
1 Stockton Street, San Francisco, CA 94102

Saeed Al Yami
5656 Bay Street, Emeryville, CA 94608

Chen Young
1823 4th Street, Berkeley, CA 94710

Jennifer Thompson
1129 Main Street, Walnut Creek, CA 94596

Figure 5.17 The finished table view cells

4. As it stands right now, there's not much of a clear division between cells in the table view. To change this, click on the gray area below the table view to select it. Then go to the Attributes Inspector and change the **Separator** setting to **Single Line**. This displays a thin line between each cell as shown in Figure 5.18.

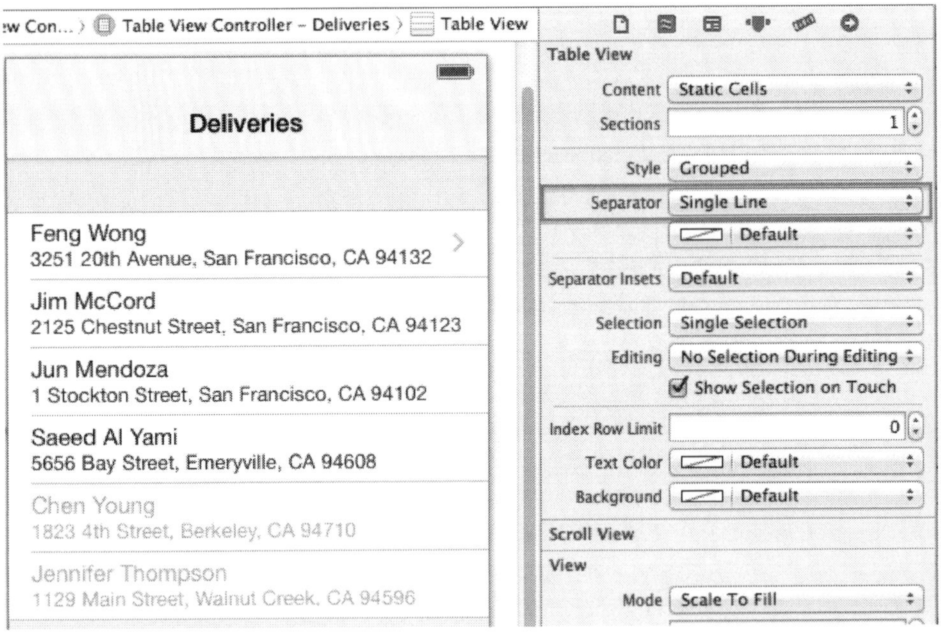

*Figure 5.18 Set the **Separator** attribute to **Single Line**.*

Toggling Retina 4 Form Factor

At the bottom of the storyboard is a rounded-rectangle button that allows you to switch all scenes on the storyboard between the Retina 3.5-inch and the Retina 4-inch form factor (Figure 5.19).

Figure 5.19 Switching between form factors

This switch allows you to see how your scenes look in each form factor. I'm going to set the storyboard to the 3.5-inch form factor (and you can do the same) so the scenes take up less space in the storyboard.

Running the Deliveries Scene

To see how the app looks at run time:

1. Press the **Run** button in Xcode. After several seconds you should see the app running in the simulator (Figure 5.20) and feel the thrill of success (if you're not feeling the thrill, check out the movie link at the end of this chapter that shows you how to perform each step by means of high quality video and narration)!

*Figure 5.20 The **Deliveries** scene running in the Simulator*

2. Go back to Xcode, and click the **Stop** button to stop the app from running in

the Simulator.

Now you're ready to move on to the next chapter where you will create the Shipment scene.

Summary

- The Interface Builder editor is automatically opened in the main workspace window when you select a user interface file in the Project Navigator.

- The Document Outline provides a hierarchical view of all UI objects on the currently selected scene.

- After creating a prototype cell, you can make copies of that cell by pressing **Command+D** (duplicate).

Step-By-Step Movie 5.1

In case you missed any of the steps along the way, go to the following link in your web browser to see each step performed for you.

http://www.iOSAppsForNonProgrammers.com/B1M51.7.html

Chapter 6: Designing the Shipment Scene

Better grab a cup!

In this chapter you will create a new Shipment scene and create a transition from the Deliveries scene to the new Shipment scene. Along the way you will learn more about storyboards, segues and working with the Attributes Inspector.

Sections in This Chapter

The Game Plan

In the previous chapter you created a Deliveries scene that displays a list of deliveries to be made. When the user selects an item from the Deliveries scene, a new scene should appear displaying details regarding the selected shipment. Figure 6.1 shows what the Shipment scene will look like when you have completed the steps in this chapter.

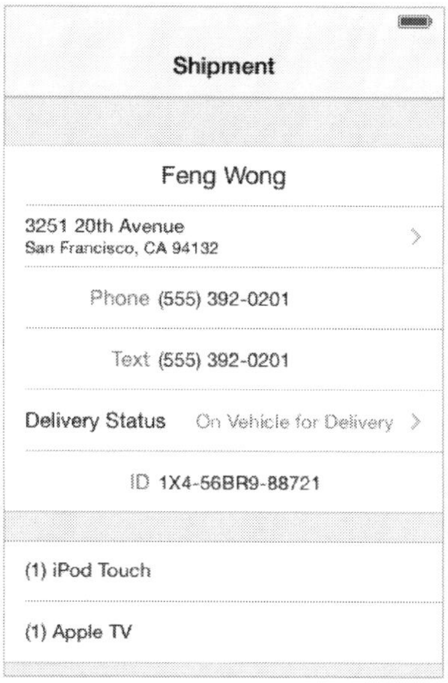

Figure 6.1 The completed Shipment scene

Since this is a prototype app, it's only necessary to have one of the items in the Deliveries list trigger this transition to the Shipment scene. The first item in the list is a good choice since most users will tend to select it.

Let's get started.

Adding a Table View Controller

Let's start by setting up the customer information section at the top of the scene in Figure 6.1.

1. If it's not already open, in Xcode, open the **iDeliverMobile** project.

2. Select the **MainStoryboard.storyboard** file in the Project Navigator if it's not already selected.

3. When adding a new scene to a storyboard, I find it helpful to zoom out of the storyboard to provide more empty space for dropping in the new scene. To do this, you can either double-click the background of the storyboard, or click the minus (-) magnifying glass icon in the bottom right of the storyboard.

4. Next, find the **Table View Controller** in the Object Library at the bottom right of the Xcode window. Drag the **Table View Controller** from the Object Library and drop it on an empty space in the storyboard (Figure 6.2).

*Figure 6.2 Drop a **Table View Controller** on the storyboard.*

5. It's best to place the scenes on the storyboard in the order in which they appear in the app. That makes it easier to see at a glance which scene comes first, second, third, and so on. To do this, select the new Table View Controller scene, then drag and drop it to the right of the Deliveries scene (Figure 6.3).

Figure 6.3 Placing the table view controller

Creating a Segue

One of the signature features of iOS is animated transitions between different views. For example, when the user taps a specific UI object, the current view is moved out of the way using ***animations*** such as sliding, curling, and dissolving, and another view replaces it.

As already mentioned, a *segue* is a visual object in a storyboard that defines transitions between different scenes. A segue allows you to specify the UI control that fires the transition, the type of transition, and the view that is moved into place as the new current view.

Let's create a segue between the first item in the Deliveries list to the new Table View Controller scene.

1. Double-click the storyboard to zoom back in.

2. To create a segue between the two scenes, follow these steps:

   • Hold the **Control** key down,

   • Click on the first cell in the **Deliveries** table view,

   • Drag over to the table view in the new scene and release the mouse button (Figure 6.4).

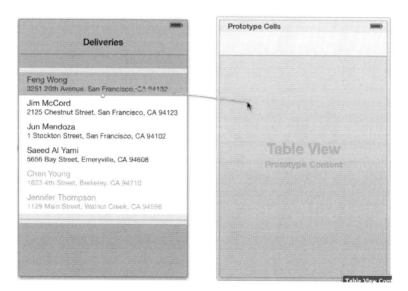

*Figure 6.4 Click and drag from the **Deliveries** table view to the new scene.*

3. When you release the mouse button, a **Selection Segue** popup appears

(Figure 6.5). Select the **push** option. This creates a transition where the Deliveries scene slides to the left and the new scene slides left to replace it.

Figure 6.5 The Selection Segue popup

There are a few things to note (Figure 6.6):

- In the Deliveries scene on the left, a disclosure indicator has been added to the right side of the first cell. This indicates to the user that tapping the cell takes them to another view. Since this is currently the only cell that takes the user to the next scene, we won't add disclosure indicators to the other cells.

- There is a new segue between the two scenes with a large gray arrow pointing from the Deliveries scene to the new scene.

- In the scene on the right, a navigation bar has been added to the top of the view. This is because the Deliveries scene on the left has a navigation bar and the new scene needs one in order to navigate back to the Deliveries scene (you will see how that works in just a bit).

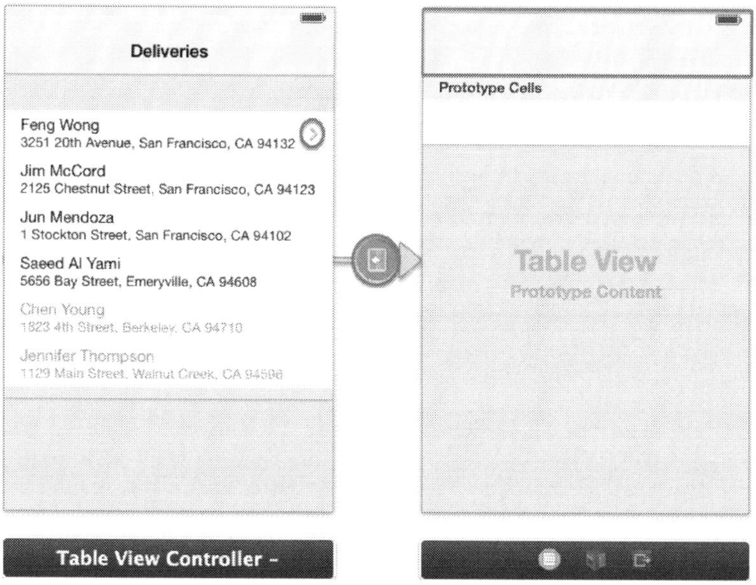

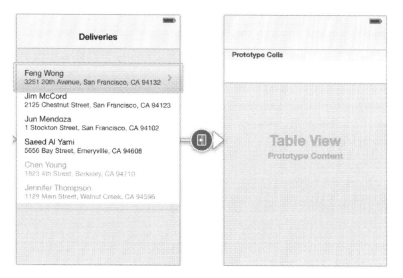

Figure 6.6 The new segue

If you look closely inside the segue (you can tap the figure to display it in full screen mode), you can see an icon with a small white arrow pointing back from the new scene to the Deliveries scene. This icon is used to indicate the segue is a "push" type where the scenes slide to the left.

4. Now click directly on the segue. Notice when you do this, the first cell in the Deliveries table view is highlighted (Figure 6.7). This is a visual design-time indicator showing you that the first cell triggers the segue transition to the next scene.

Figure 6.7 Select the segue.

Setting Up the Shipment Scene

Now that you have set up a segue between the two scenes, it's time to set up the Shipment scene. Let's start by changing the title of the scene's navigation bar.

1. Double-click the new scene's navigation bar and type the title **Shipment** as shown in Figure 6.8. Press **Enter** to complete the change to the title.

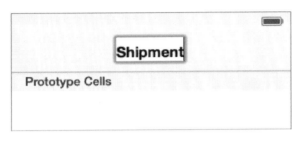

Figure 6.8 Change the navigation bar title.

2. Next, in the Document Outline pane, select the Shipment scene's **Table View** as shown in Figure 6.9. If you don't see the Document Outline pane, select the rounded-rectangle arrow button at the bottom left of the Interface Builder editor, or select **Editor > Show Document Outline** from the Xcode menu.

*Figure 6.9 Select the Shipment Scene's **Table View**.*

3. In the Attributes Inspector's **Table View** section, change the **Content** to **Static Cells**. This adds three static cells to the table view (Figure 6.10).

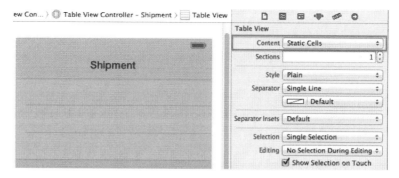

*Figure 6.10 Change the **Content** to **Static Cells**.*

Most of the table view cells will be formatted differently, so let's just leave the three cells in place.

4. A little further down in the Attributes Inspector, set the **Style** attribute to **Grouped**.

5. When you change the **Grouped** setting, Xcode automatically changes the **Separator** setting. To get the original setting back again, change the **Separator** setting to **Single Line**.

6. The table view needs two sections, so let's create the second section now. To do this, go to the **Sections** setting and click the up arrow to set the section count to **2** as shown in Figure 6.11.

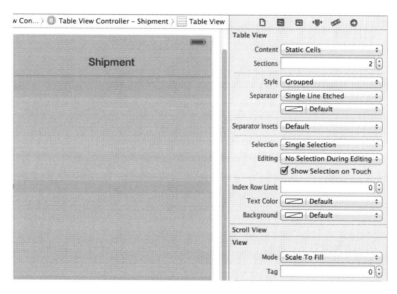

Figure 6.11 The Shipment table view with two sections

7. You only need two cells in the second section, so select the last cell in the second section and press the **Delete** key. This leaves three cells in the first

section and two in the second (Figure 6.12).

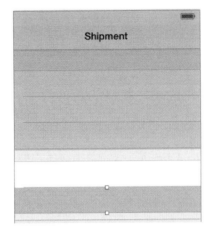

Figure 6.12 Two cells left in the second section

Setting Up the Customer Name

Now let's set up the first cell in the first table view section. This cell will contain the customer's name.

1. Select the first cell in the table view as shown in Figure 6.13.

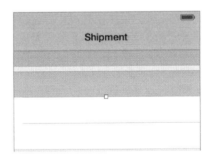

Figure 6.13 Select the first cell in the table view.

2. In the Attributes Inspector's **Table View Cell** section, change the **Style** to **Basic**. This adds a single left-aligned text label to the cell (Figure 6.14).

*Figure 6.14 Set the cell **Style** to **Basic**.*

3. With the first cell still selected, click on the cell two more times. This selects the new label inside of the cell. With the label selected, go to the Attributes Inspector and set the **Text** to **Feng Wong**, or whichever name you set in the first cell of the Deliveries table view controller.

4. Next, set the **Alignment** to center-aligned. This places the label in the middle of the cell (Figure 6.15).

Figure 6.15 Set the label to center-aligned.

Setting Up the Customer Address

Now let's set up the second cell in the table view. This cell contains the customer's address. Since there is a lot of information to display, we can use two lines of the cell to display address, city, region, and postal code.

1. Select the second cell in the design surface by clicking on it. Next, go to the Attributes Inspector and change the cell's **Style** to **Subtitle**.

2. In the next chapter, you are going to set up this cell so that when the user taps the row at runtime, they are taken to a map showing a pin that represents the customer's location.

For now, you need to add a disclosure indicator to provide an indication that something happens when the user taps this row. Although a disclosure indicator is added automatically when you create a segue between the cell and a view controller, I'd like you to see how to add it to the cell manually. To do this, with the cell still selected, go to the Attributes Inspector and change the **Accessory** setting to **Disclosure Indicator**. This displays a grey disclosure indicator arrow to the right of the cell (Figure 6.16).

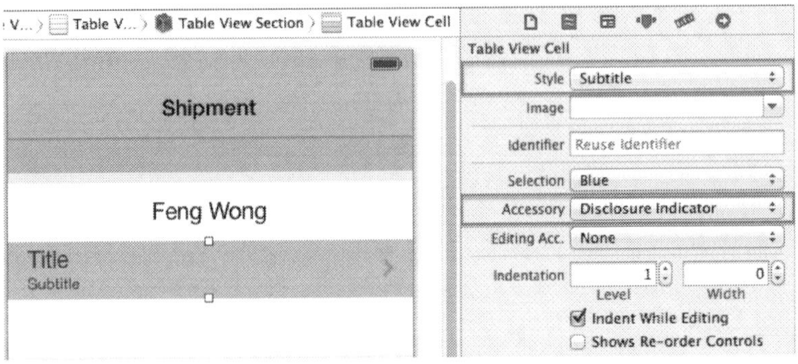

Figure 6.16 Setting the **Style** and **Accessory** type

3. With the second cell still selected, click on the cell again to select the cell's **Title** label, and then double-click it *again* to put the label in edit mode. Change the text to **3251 20th Avenue** (change it directly in the label, not in the Attributes Inspector—otherwise the text gets truncated).

   Now go to the **Font** setting, and click the down arrow to change the font size to **14**.

   Next, double-click the **Subtitle** label to put it in edit mode, and change its text to **San Francisco, CA 94132** (type directly in the label). When you're finished, click anywhere else in the editor off of the second cell, and the cell will look like Figure 6.17.

Figure 6.17 The completed second cell

4. Before continuing, let's create a few empty cells that can be used later on. To do this, select the third cell, and then press **Command+D** twice to create

two new empty cells. When you're finished, the first section of the table view will look like Figure 6.18.

Figure 6.18 Creating new empty cells

Setting Up Phone and Text Cells

Now let's set up the third and fourth cells in the table view that contain the customer's phone and text information. Since these cells are similar, you can set up the third cell that contains the phone number and then duplicate the cell for the text number.

1. Select the third cell in the table view. Go to the Attributes Inspector and change the **Style** to **Left Detail**. This adds two labels to the cell: A small blue **Title** label and a larger, black **Detail** label as shown in Figure 6.19.

*Figure 6.19 Set the third cell's **Style** to **Detail**.*

2. With the third cell still selected, click twice to select the blue **Title** label on the left. Go to the Attributes Inspector and change the following attributes:

    •   Set the **Text** attribute to **Phone**.

- Set the **Font Size** to **15**.

3. Next, double-click the **Detail** label in the third cell and change its **Text** to **(555) 392-0201** (enter the text directly into the label).

4. You can click anywhere else in the design surface to end editing of the label. When you're finished, the third cell of the table view should look like Figure 6.20.

Figure 6.20 The completed third cell

5. Since the fourth cell of the Shipment table view is similar to the third cell, let's duplicate the third cell. To do this, select the third cell in the design surface and press **Command+D** to duplicate the cell as shown in Figure 6.21.

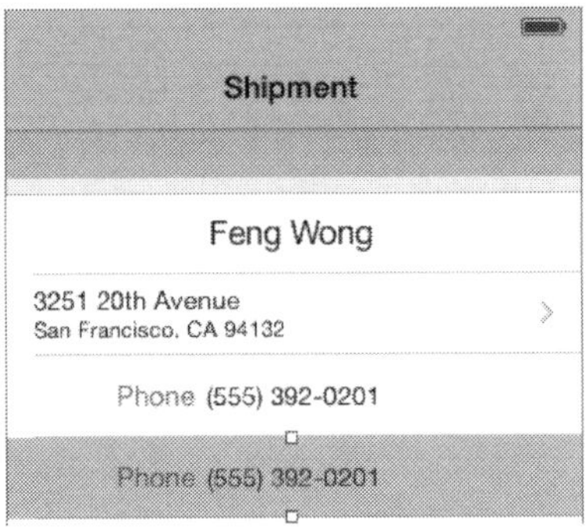

Figure 6.21 Duplicate the third cell.

6. Now you're ready to change the label text of the fourth cell. With the cell selected, click twice to select the **Phone** label, go to the Attributes Inspector and set the **Text** attribute to **Text** (funny, I know). You can leave the phone number set to its current value. When you're finished, click anywhere else in the design surface to deselect the fourth cell, which should now look like Figure 6.22.

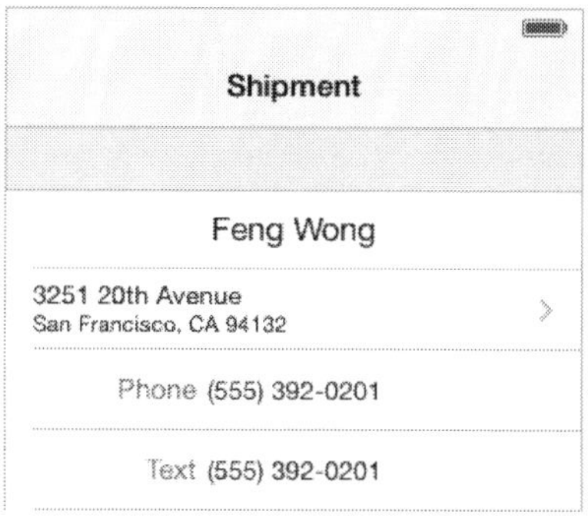

*Figure 6.22 The completed **Text** cell*

Setting Up the Delivery Status Cell

Now it's time to set up the fifth cell in the Shipment table view. This cell contains the shipment's delivery status. When the user taps this cell, it takes them to the Delivery Status scene, which you will create in an upcoming chapter. So, this cell also needs a disclosure indicator.

1. Select the fifth cell in the table view, and then go to the Attributes Inspector. Change the **Style** of the cell to **Right Detail**, and then set the **Accessory** to **Disclosure Indicator** (Figure 6.23).

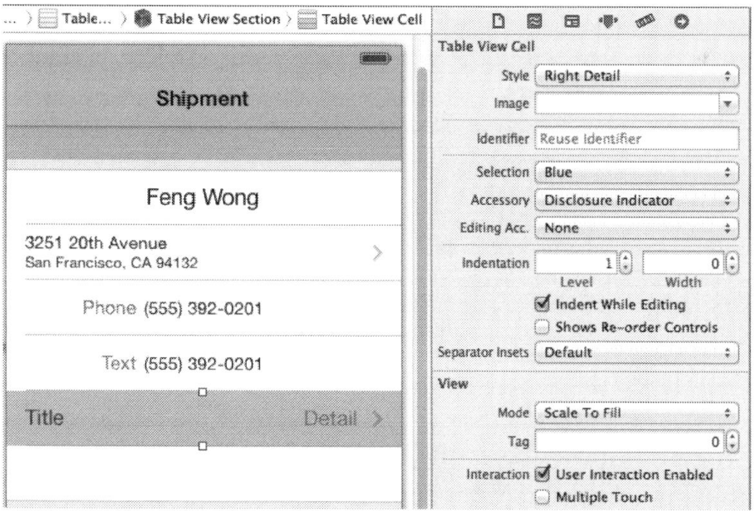

*Figure 6.23 Set the **Style** to **Right Detail** and **Accessory** to **Disclosure Indicator**.*

2. Next, double-click the **Title** label in the fifth cell to put it into edit mode, and change the **Text** to **Delivery Status**. With the label still selected, change the **Font Size** to **15**.
3. Double-click the **Detail** label in the fifth cell to put it into edit mode, and

75

change the text to **On Vehicle for Delivery**. With the label still selected, change the **Font Size** to **14**.

When you're finished, click anywhere else in the design surface to deselect the fifth cell ,which should now look like Figure 6.24.

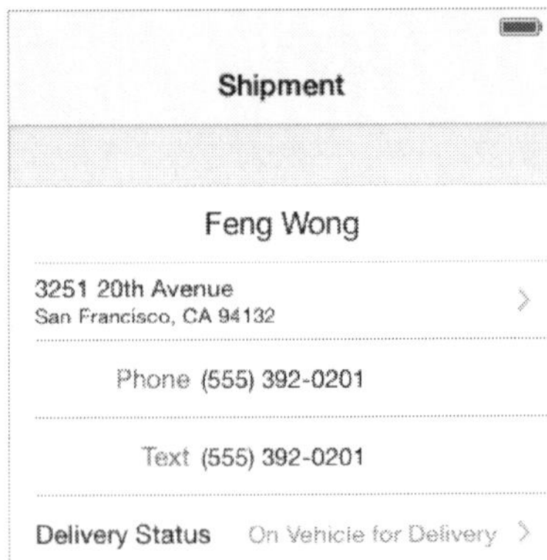

Shipment

Feng Wong

3251 20th Avenue
San Francisco, CA 94132   >

Phone (555) 392-0201

Text (555) 392-0201

Delivery Status   On Vehicle for Delivery >

*Figure 6.24 The completed **Delivery Status** cell*

Setting Up the Shipment ID Cell

There is one more cell left to set up in the first section of the Shipment table view—the Shipment ID cell.

1. Select the sixth (last) cell in the table view. In the Attributes Inspector, set the **Style** to **Left Detail**. This adds **Title** and **Subtitle** labels to the cell.

2. Select the **Title** label, and then set the following attributes in the Attribute Inspector:

   • Set the **Text** attribute to **ID**.

   • Set the **Font Size** to **15**.

3. Double-click the **Detail** label to put it into edit mode and change the text to **1X4-56BR9-88721** (or any other name you like—it's just a fake ID number that looks impressive). You can leave the font setting at the default value

When you're finished, the sixth table view cell should look like Figure 6.25.

ID 1X4-56BR9-88721

Figure 6.25 The completed Shipment ID cell

Setting Up the Shipment Detail Section

Now you're ready to set up the shipment detail section of the Shipment table view. Previously, when there were multiple cells with similar styles, you created one cell, and then copied the cell to create the next. In this section, you will learn how to change two cells at the same time.

1. Select both cells in the second section. To do this, click on the first cell, hold down the **Shift** key and click the second cell. With both cells selected, go to the Attributes Inspector and change the **Style** to **Basic** (Figure 6.26).

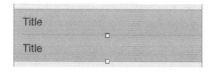

*Figure 6.26 Set the **Style** to **Basic** on both cells.*

When you have multiple cells selected, you can change all of the attributes at the cell level at the same time such as Style, Accessory, Interaction, and Background. However, if you need to change attributes of the labels or other controls contained within a cell, you need to edit them separately as you will do in the next step.

2. Select the first cell in the second section. This automatically deselects the second cell. Click on the first cell two more times to edit the label inside the cell, and then set the following attributes in the Attributes Inspector:

   • Set the **Text** to **(1) iPod Touch**.

   • Set the **Font Size** to **14**.

3. Select the second cell in the second section. Click on the cell a second time to edit the label inside the cell, then set the following attributes:

   • Set the **Text** to **(1) Apple TV**.

   • Set the **Font** to **System**.

   • Set the **Font Size** to **14**.

4. When you're finished, click anywhere else in the design surface to deselect the table view cell.

The second table view section should   look like Figure 6.27.

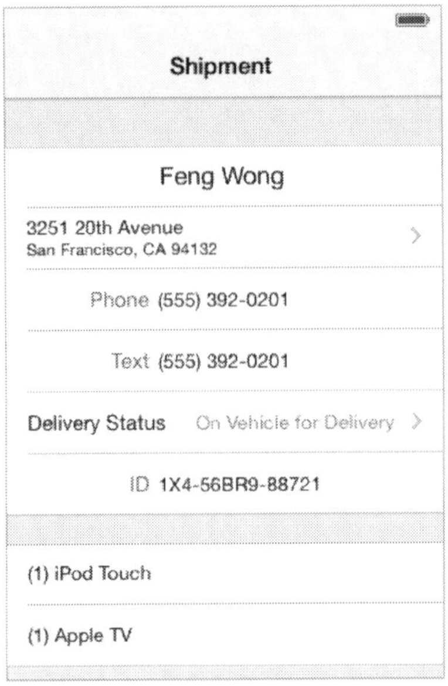

Figure 6.27 The completed Shipment table view

Testing the Shipment Scene

To see how the Shipment scene works at run time, click the **Run** button in Xcode. You should see the first **Deliveries** scene, and then you can select the first delivery in the list to see the **Shipment** scene.

As shown in Figure 6.28, the **Shipment** scene has a "back button" on the left side of its navigation bar at the top of the screen that you don't see at design time.

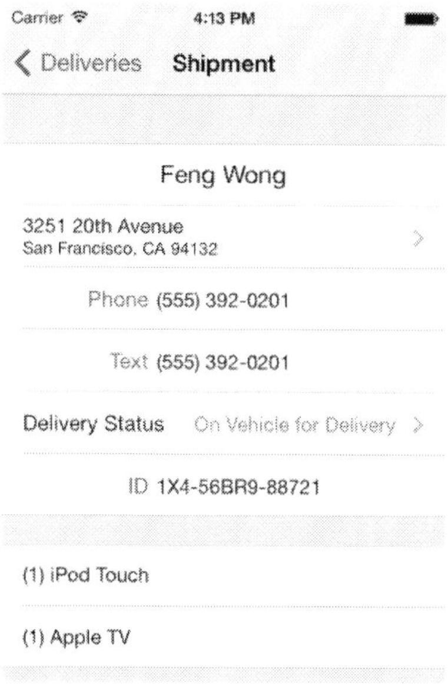

Figure 6.28 The Shipment scene at run time

This button is automatically added for you, and by default it contains the header text of the previous scene (in this case, **Deliveries**). If you tap this button, it takes you back to the Deliveries scene.

When you're finished admiring your new accomplishment, go back to Xcode and press the **Stop** button to stop the app from running in the Simulator.

Summary

- In Xcode, you can double-click the storyboard to zoom in and zoom out, or you can click the plus and minus buttons in the bottom right corner of the Interface Builder.

- It's best to place the scenes on the storyboard in the order in which they appear in the app. That makes it easier to see at a glance which scene comes first, second, third, and so on.

- A *segue* is a visual object in a storyboard that defines transitions between different scenes. A segue allows you to specify the UI control that fires the transition, the type of transition, and the view that is moved into place as the new current view.

- To duplicate an object in Interface Builder, select the object and press **Command+D**.

- To select multiple objects in Interface Builder, click on one object, hold the **Shift** key down and click on one or more other objects.

Step-By-Step Movie 6.1

In case you missed any of the steps along the way, go to the following link in your web browser to see each step performed for you.

http://www.iOSAppsForNonProgrammers.com/B1M61.7.html

Chapter 7: Adding a Map & User Location

In this section you are going to add a new Location scene to the storyboard, connect it to the address cell by means of a segue, and then add a map to the view that can be used to show the customer's location.

Sections in This Chapter

1. *Begin With the End in Mind*

2. *Adding the Location View Controller*

3. *Adding a Segue to the Location Scene*

4. *Setting Up the Location Scene*

5. *Summary*

6. *Step-By-Step Movie 7.1*

Begin With the End in Mind

When the user taps the address in the first section of the Shipment table view, it displays the user's location on a map. Figure 7.1 shows how this will look when you're finished.

Figure 7.1 The finished Location scene

We won't be adding the toolbar with the page curl button to the bottom of the scene in this section, but will wait until a later chapter.

Adding the Location View Controller

Rather than adding a table view controller, you are going to add a regular view controller for the Location scene because the Location scene doesn't contain a table view!

1. If it's not already open, in Xcode, open the **iDeliverMobile** project.

2. Select the **MainStoryboard.storyboard** file in the Project Navigator.

3. Double-click the storyboard to zoom out, or click the minus (-) zoom button in the bottom right corner of the Interface Builder pane.

4. From the Object Library, drag a **View Controller** and drop it on the storyboard as shown in Figure 7.2.

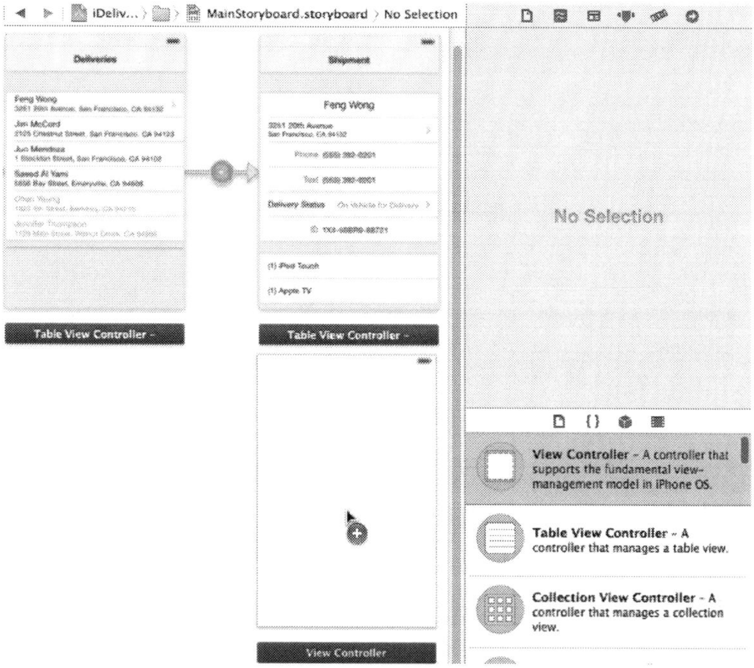

*Figure 7.2 Drop a **View Controller** on the storyboard.*

5. Again, I like to position the scenes in the order in which they are appear in the app. So, let's drag the new scene and drop it to the right of the Shipment scene (Figure 7.3).

Figure 7.3 Position the new view controller.

6. Before doing anything else, zoom back in on the storyboard. To do this, just double-click the storyboard or click the plus (+) zoom button.

Adding a Segue to the Location Scene

Now lets add a segue that connects the address cell of the **Shipment** table view to the new scene.

1. In the **Shipment** table view, click the address cell, hold down the **Control** key and then drag over to the new scene (Figure 7.4).

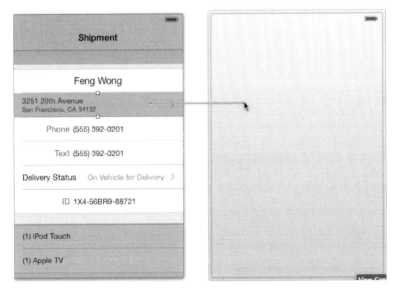

Figure 7.4 **Control+Drag** *to create a connection to the new scene.*

2. When you release the mouse, the Storyboard Segues popup appears. In the popup, select the **push** option again. This adds a segue between the two scenes and a navigation bar to the top of the new scene (Figure 7.5).

Figure 7.5 A segue between the address cell and the new scene

Setting Up the Location Scene

Now that you have set up a segue between the Shipment and Location scenes, it's time to set up the Location scene. Let's start by changing the title of the scene's navigation bar.

1. Double-click the navigation bar in the new scene, enter the text **Location** and press **Enter** (Figure 7.6).

*Figure 7.6 Set the title of the new scene to **Location**.*

2. Now let's add a map view control to the Location scene. Scroll down in the Object Library until you see the **Map View** control. Click the **Map View** in the Object Library, and then drag it over to the **Location** scene. Hover the map view over the center of the scene until you see the horizontal and vertical guide lines appear (Figure 7.7) and then release the mouse.

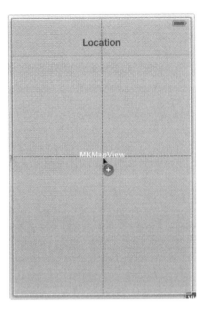

Figure 7.7 Hover the map view over the scene's center.

This causes the map view to fill all of the available space in the view, which is exactly what we want. When we eventually convert the prototype app to a fully-functioning app, when the user taps the map, the navigation bar can be automatically hidden, and the map will fill the entire screen.

3. With the map view still selected, go to the Attributes Inspector under the **Map View** section and select the **Shows User Location** check box as shown in Figure 7.8.

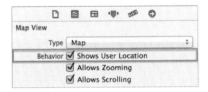

*Figure 7.8 Select the **Shows User Location** option.*

This tells the map view to automatically show the user's current location when the map is displayed at run time.

Rather than write code to display the location of the selected customer (since this *is* a prototype), we are simply going to use the user's current location.

Adding the MapKit Framework

Whenever you add a map view to your app's user interface, you need to take an additional step and add the Cocoa Touch **MapKit** framework to your project. If you don't do this, you will get a "Could not instantiate class named MKMapView" error when you try to display the map at run time.

1. To add the MapKit framework, go to the Project Navigator and select the very first node in the list (the project node). When you select this node, Xcode displays the Project Editor (Figure 7.9).

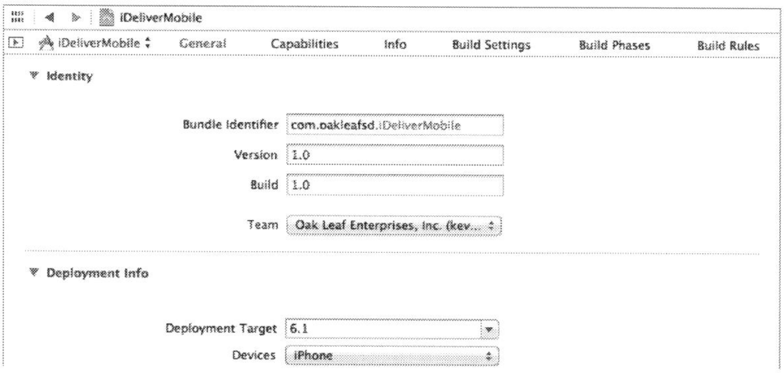

Figure 7.9 The Project Editor

2. With the **iDeliverMobile** target selected in the pane on the left, scroll down in the project editor on the right until you see the **Linked Frameworks and Libraries** section (Figure 7.10).

*Figure 7.10 **Linked Frameworks and Libraries***

3. Click the plus (+) sign at the bottom left of the Linked Frameworks and Libraries section. This displays the Frameworks and Libraries dialog (Figure 7.11). Scroll down until you see **MapKit.framework**. Select this item and then click the **Add** button to add the MapKit framework to the project.

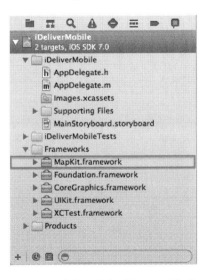

*Figure 7.11 Add **MapKit.framework** to the project.*

4. This adds the **MapKit.framework** beneath the Frameworks group in the Project Navigator as shown in Figure 7.12.

*Figure 7.12 **MapKit.framework** is added beneath the **Frameworks** group.*

Testing the Map Scene

Now let's see what the map looks like at run time.

1. In Xcode, click the **Run** button to run the app in the Simulator. When the first scene appears, pick the first delivery in the list. This takes you to the **Shipment** scene. Select the address row and this will take you to the

Location scene. You will see an alert asking if you will allow iDeliverMobile to use your current location (Figure 7.13). This alert is automatically displayed by iOS whenever an app requests the user's current location.

Figure 7.13 iOS asks if you will allow iDeliverMobile to use your current location.

2. Click **OK** and your "current location" is displayed on the map. Since you are not running on a real iOS device, by default, the map displays Apple headquarters at One Infinite Loop as your current location (Figure 7.14) unless you have previously changed the Location setting in the Simulator. If you don't see Apple headquarters, just select **Debug > Location > Apple** from the Simulator menu.

Figure 7.14 One Infinite Loop is your default location.

As you can see in Figure 7.14, the map does not zoom into the current location by default. To do this, you need to write some code, which we won't do right now.

3. You can change the default location in the Simulator. To do this, select **Debug > Location** from the iOS Simulator's menu. This displays a Custom Location dialog you can use to enter a different latitude and longitude. I have determined the real latitude and longitude of the address you have selected for the delivery to Feng Wong (3251 20th Avenue, San Francisco, CA 94132) by using the www.FindLatitudeAndLongitude.com web site. To set this address as the current location, in the **Latitude** box, enter **37.729133**, and in the **Longitude** box, enter **-122.476728** as shown in Figure 7.15. Afterwards, click **OK**.

Figure 7.15 Enter a custom latitude and longitude.

4. Even though the map doesn't automatically zoom into the current location, you can zoom in manually by double-clicking on the map. You should first position the blue location dot in the middle of the Simulator screen by

clicking and dragging, and then begin double-clicking. You can zoom in to see all the street detail you need (Figure 7.16).

Figure 7.16 Zoom in by double clicking.

5. Go back to Xcode and press the **Stop** button to stop the app from running in the Simulator.

This completes the setup of the Location scene! End users love to have maps that show their current location or the location of places they are looking for. If you can find a way to incorporate location technology in your app, I highly recommend that you do it!

Summary

- If a scene doesn't contain a table view controller, you can drag a View Controller object onto the storyboard instead.

- Showing the user's current location is as easy as selecting the map view control and selecting its **Shows User Location** check box in the Attributes Inspector.

- Whenever you add a map view to your app's user interface, you need to take an additional step and add the Cocoa Touch **MapKit** framework to your project.

- Since Xcode doesn't automatically place newly added frameworks under the

Frameworks group, you should click and drag newly added frameworks down to the **Frameworks** group.

- iOS automatically displays an alert whenever an app requests the user's current location.

- You can specify a different "user location" by selecting **Debug > Location** from the Simulator's menu.

Step-By-Step Movie 7.1

In case you missed any of the steps along the way, go to the following link in your web browser to see each step performed for you.

http://www.iOSAppsForNonProgrammers.com/B1M71.7.html

Chapter 8: Showing Shipment Status

In this chapter, as you create the Delivery Status scene, you will learn more about creating table views with static content and find out how to create a table view where the user can select one of several items.

Sections in This Chapter

1. *The Completed Scene*

2. *Adding a Table View Controller*

3. *Setting Up the Table View Controller*

4. *Setting the Table View Background Color*

5. *Testing the Delivery Status Scene*

6. *Step-By-Step Movie 8.1*

The Completed Scene

As mentioned earlier, when the user taps the Delivery Status row in the first section of the Shipment table view, the app navigates to another scene where the user can change the delivery status. In this section, you are going to add a new view controller and view to the storyboard, connect it to the Delivery Status cell by means of a segue, and then add a table view from which the user can select a delivery status.

As always, let's take a look at the completed scene so we know where we're headed (Figure 8.1).

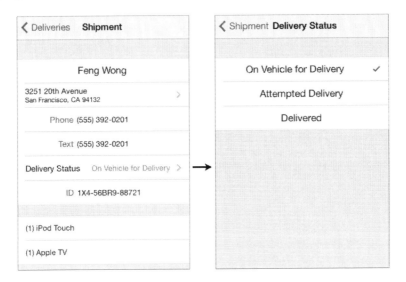

Figure 8.1 The completed scene

Adding a Table View Controller

1. Open the **iDeliverMobile** project in Xcode and select the **MainStoryboard.storyboard** file.

2. Double-click the storyboard background to zoom out, or click the minus (-) zoom button.

3. From the Object Library, drag a **Table View Controller** and drop it on the storyboard below the **Location** scene (Figure 8.2).

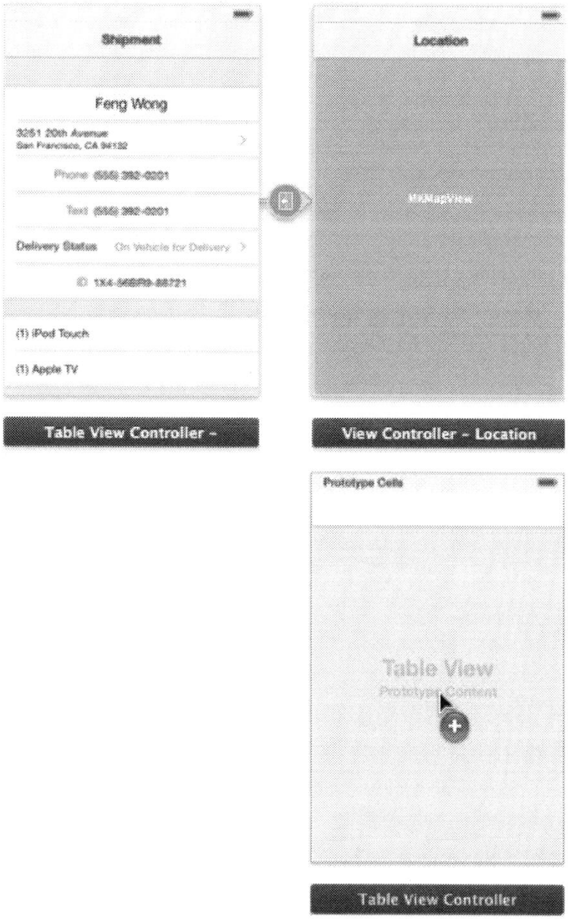

Figure 8.2 Add a table view controller to the storyboard.

I have placed the new scene under the **Location** scene because they are peers in the scene hierarchy—meaning, they are both launched from the **Shipment** scene.

Adding a Segue to the New Scene

1. Double-click the storyboard to zoom back in. Next, hold the **Control** key down, click on the **Delivery Status** cell in the **Shipment** scene and drag down to the new scene as shown in Figure 8.3.

95

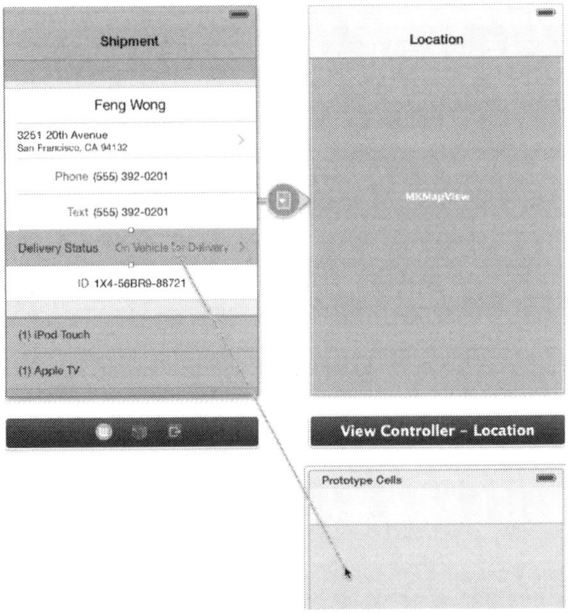

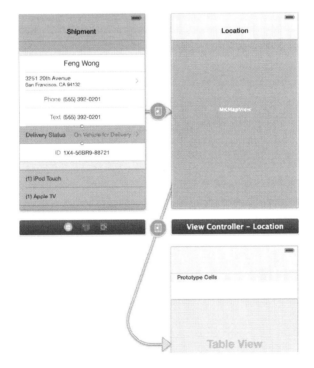

Figure 8.3 Create a segue to the new scene.

2. Let go of the mouse to display the **Selection Segue** popup. In the popup, select the **push** option. This creates a segue from the **Shipment** scene and adds a navigation bar to the top of the **Delivery Status** scene as shown in Figure 8.4.

Figure 8.4 The newly added segue

Setting Up the Table View Controller

Now you're ready to set up the Delivery Status table view controller.

1. Double-click the navigation bar at the top of the new scene and set the title to **Delivery Status** as shown in Figure 8.5.

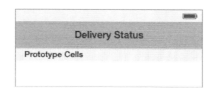

*Figure 8.5 Set the title to **Delivery Status**.*

2. In the Document Outline pane, in the **Delivery Status** scene, select the **Table View** as shown in Figure 8.6.

*Figure 8.6 Select the **Delivery Status Scene's Table View**.*

3. With the table view selected, go to the Attributes Inspector and set the following attributes:

- Set **Content** to **Static Cells**.

- Set **Style** to **Grouped**.

- Set **Separator** to **Single Line**.

When you're finished, the Delivery Status table view should look like Figure 8.7.

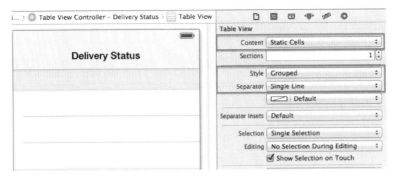

*Figure 8.7 Set the **Content**, **Style**, and **Separator** attributes.*

Setting Up the Delivery Status Cells

All three cells in the Delivery Status table view need to be the same style, so it's easiest to delete the last two cells, set up the first cell, and then make two copies.

1. Select the last two cells in the Delivery Status table view—just click the second cell, hold the **Shift** key down and click the third cell. With both cells selected, press the **Delete** key. This leaves just one cell in the table view (Figure 8.8).

Figure 8.8 Leave just one cell in the table view.

2. With the only cell in the table view selected, go to the Attributes Inspector and set the **Style** to **Basic**. This adds a **Title** label on the left side of the cell (Figure 8.9).

*Figure 8.9 Set the **Style** to **Basic**.*

3. With the cell still selected, click the cell twice to select the newly added label. Set the following attributes in the Attributes Inspector:

    •   Set the **Text** to **On Vehicle for Delivery**.

- Set the **Alignment** to center-aligned.

When you're finished, the cell should look like Figure 8.10.

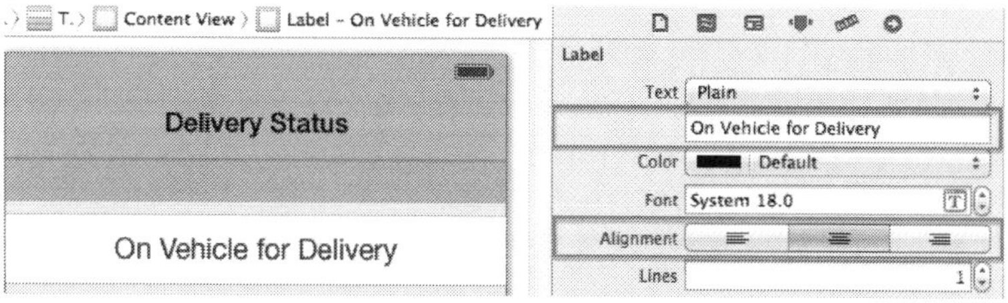

Figure 8.10 The formatted Delivery Status table view cell

4. Now let's make two copies of the cell. To do this, click anywhere else on the storyboard, click the cell to select it again, and then press **Command+D** twice. This creates two additional cells (Figure 8.11).

Figure 8.11 Create two duplicates of the first cell.

5. Now let's add the finishing touches to these cells. In the real app, the user will be able to select an item from this list, and the selected item will display a check mark. In the prototype, we will simply mark the first cell in the table view with a check mark.

Select the first cell, go to the Attributes Inspector and change the **Accessory** setting to **Checkmark**. This displays a check mark on the right side of the cell (Figure 8.12).

*Figure 8.12 Set the **Accessory** attribute to **Checkmark**.*

6. Next, click the second cell to select it, and then click it twice more to edit the label within the cell. Go to the Attributes Inspector and change the **Text** to **Attempted Delivery**.

7. Do the same to the third cell, but change the label's **Text** to **Delivered**. When you're finished, the three cells should look like Figure 8.13.

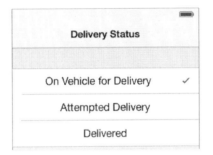

Figure 8.13 The completed Delivery Status table view

Testing the Delivery Status Scene

Now you're ready to see how the Delivery Status Scene looks at run time.

1. Click the **Run** button in Xcode.

2. When the app appears in the Simulator, the Deliveries scene is displayed first. Select the first delivery in the list to see the Shipment scene.

3. Select the Delivery Status row to see the Delivery Status scene and it should look like Figure 8.14.

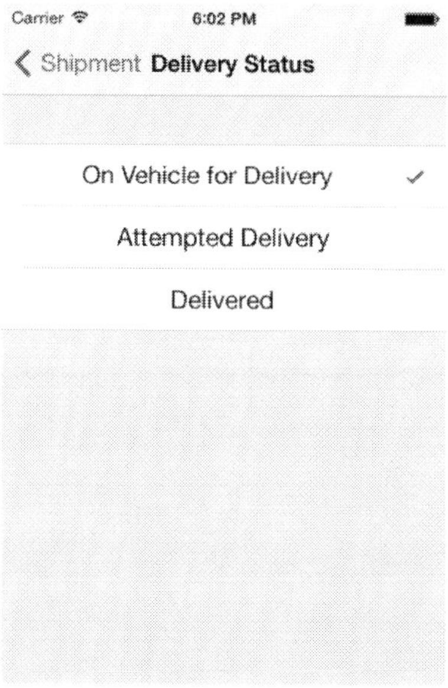

Figure 8.14 The Delivery Status scene at run time

Since this is a prototype and we haven't written any code, you won't be able to select a different status, but it gives you a very good idea of how the finished app will work.

4. Go back to Xcode and press the **Stop** button to stop the app from running in the Simulator

This completes the setup of the Delivery Status scene!

Step-By-Step Movie 8.1

In case you missed any of the steps along the way, go to the following link in your web browser to see each step performed for you.

http://www.iOSAppsForNonProgrammers.com/B1M81.7.html

Chapter 9: Providing Map Options

The road to Lahaina

As you create the Map Options scene in this chapter, you are introduced to new user-interface controls—Toolbars, Toolbar Buttons, Flexible Space Bar Button Items, and Segmented Controls. You will also learn how to create a modal segue with a partial curl transition.

Sections in This Chapter

1. *The Final Scene*

2. *Adding the Map Options View Controller*

3. *Adding a Toolbar to the Location Scene*

4. *Create a Segue to the Map Options Scene*

5. *Setting Up the Map Options Scene*

6. *Testing the Map Options Scene*

7. *Summary*

8. *Step-By-Step Movie 9.1*

The Final Scene

The steps in this chapter involve two different scenes. First, you're going to add a toolbar containing an Info button to the bottom of the Location scene as shown in Figure 9.1.

Figure 9.1 The Location scene with an Info button

When the user taps this button, the Map Options scene (Figure 9.2) slides up from the bottom of the screen.

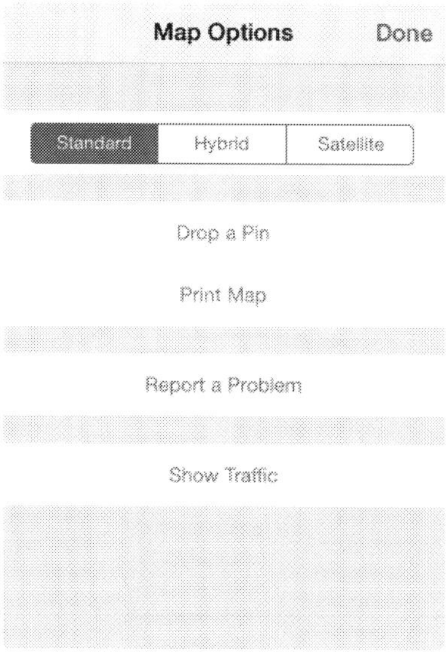

Figure 9.2 The Map Options scene

In this prototype version of the app, the options on this scene will be visible but not functional.

Adding the Map Options View Controller

This is the first time we have created a *modal* scene that slides up from the bottom of the screen. In iOS, a modal scene is usually a "dead end." The user transitions to a modal scene and back again, but the modal scene doesn't take them to another new scene. As you will see in just a bit, a scene becomes modal when you create a modal segue to that scene.

A modal segue works a little differently than a push segue in that creating a modal segue does not add a navigation bar to the top of the destination scene. Since we *do* want a navigation bar at the top of the Map Options scene, we can achieve this by adding a Navigation Controller to the storyboard, which in turn adds an associated table view controller. We can then create a segue from the Location scene to the Navigation Controller scene.

1. Open the **iDeliverMobile** project in Xcode and select the **MainStoryboard.storyboard** file.

2. Double-click the storyboard background to zoom out, or use the minus (-) zoom button.

3. From the Object Library, drag a **Navigation Controller** and drop it on any empty area of the storyboard. Since this scene is going to be called from the Location scene, let's position the new scene to the right of the **Location** scene (Figure 9.3).

4. Zoom back out of the storyboard.

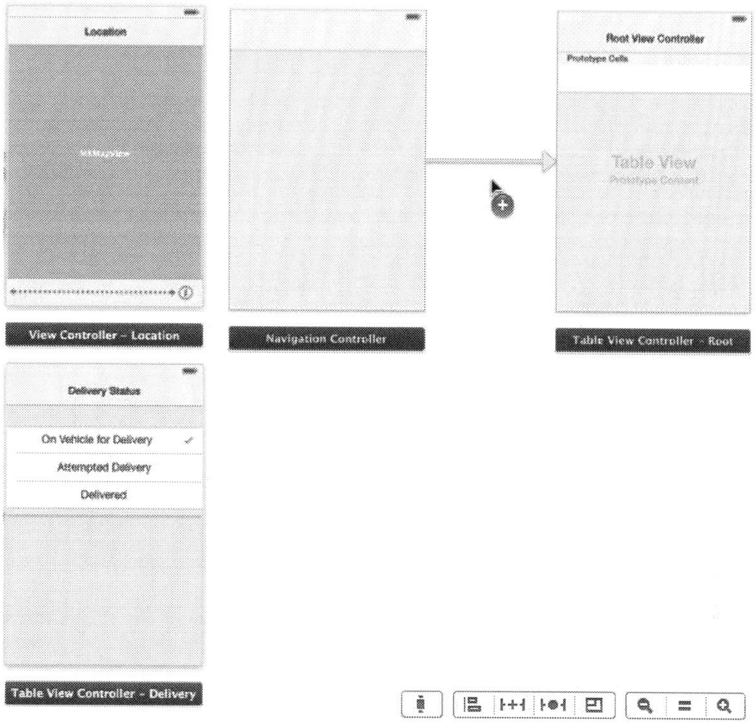

Figure 9.3 Position the new Navigation Controller.

Adding a Toolbar to the Location Scene

Next, let's add a toolbar to the bottom of the Location scene and add a button to the toolbar that launches the new Map Options scene.

1. Scroll down in the Object Library and select a **Toolbar**. Drag it over to the Location scene and place it at the very bottom of the view until it "snaps" into place. When you have positioned it correctly, you will see a blue dotted line around the view and a blue vertical guide line down the middle of the view (Figure 9.4). When you're in the right position, you can release the mouse. Again, once we transform the prototype app into a fully-functioning app, when the user taps the map, this toolbar will be hidden along with the navigation bar.

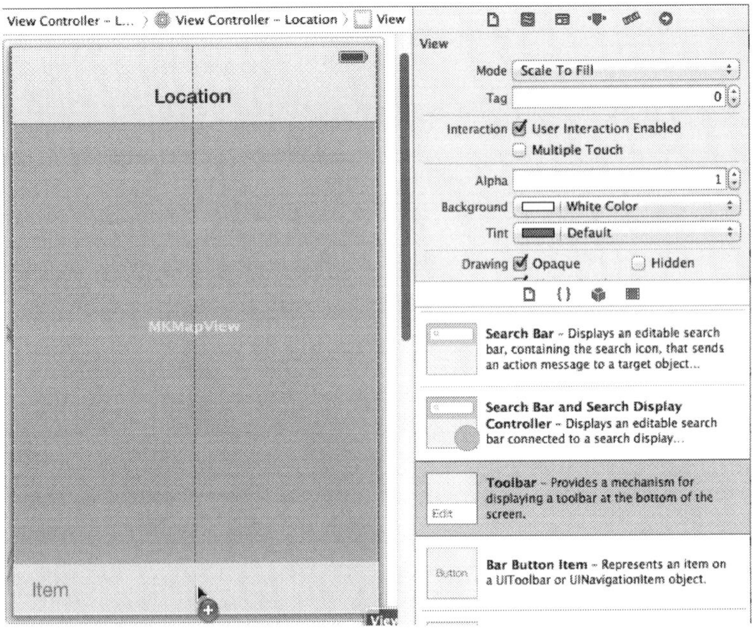

Figure 9.4 Adding a toolbar to the Location scene

2. As you can see, there is already an **Item** button included on the left side of the toolbar, but we need a different type of button because this default button can't display an **Info** button icon. So, our first step is to delete the existing button.

   To do this, click on the **Item** button to select it, and then press the **Delete** key. This removes the button from the toolbar.

3. Next, go to the Object Library, drag a **Button** (*not* a **Bar Button Item**) and drop it on the toolbar. When you do this, the button is automatically placed on the left side of the toolbar as shown in Figure 9.5.

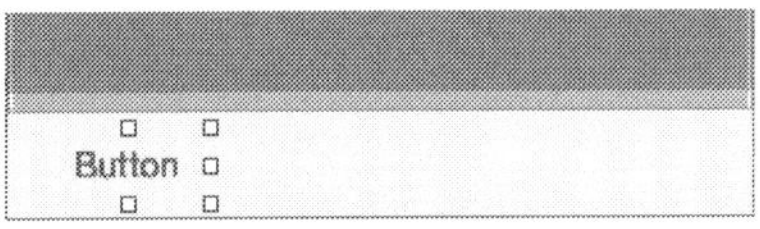

*Figure 9.5 Add a **Button** to the toolbar.*

4. If you look at the **Location Scene** in the Document Outline, you can see that when you added the **Button** to the toolbar, Xcode automatically placed it inside of a **Bar Button Item** (Figure 9.6).

*Figure 9.6 The newly added **Button** is contained within a **Bar Button Item**.*

This allow the button to be treated just as any other bar button item, but allows us to display the Info icon in the inner button.

5. Next, select the nested **Button – Button** item in the Document Outline, go to the Attributes Inspector, and set the **Type** attribute to **Info Light**. This displays the Info icon in the button on the left side of the toolbar as shown in Figure 9.7.

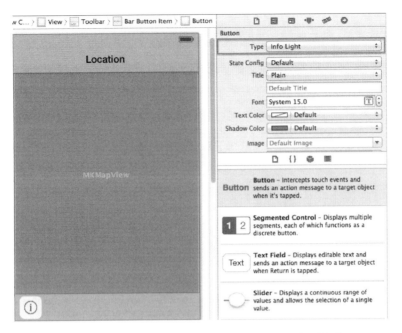

*Figure 9.7 Set the button's **Type** to **Info Light**.*

6. Starting with iOS 7, users normally expect the Info button to be located on the right side of the toolbar. If you try to click and drag the Bar Button Item to the right side of the toolbar, when you let go of the mouse, it snaps right back to the left side of the view.

    To solve this problem, you need to add a Flexible Space Bar Button Item to the toolbar. To do this, select the **Flexible Space Bar Button Item** in the Object Library, drag it over to the left of the **Item** button in the toolbar, and release the mouse button when you see the blue arrow to the left of the **Item** button (Figure 9.8).

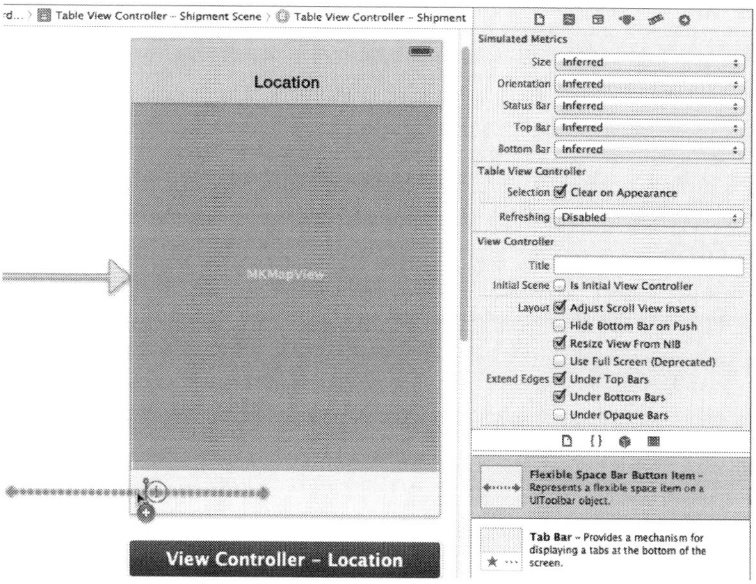

Figure 9.8 Add a **Flexible Space Bar Button Item**.

When you release the mouse button, the **Info** button is moved to the far right of the toolbar (Figure 9.9).

Figure 9.9 The Info button is moved to the right.

Create a Segue to the Map Options Scene

Now let's create a segue between the Info button and the new Map Options scene.

1. First click the toolbar to select it, and then click the Info button. Click on the button a second time to select the inner button.

2. Now, hold the **Control** key down, click on the Info button, and then drag your mouse over to the new Navigation Controller scene (Figure 9.10).

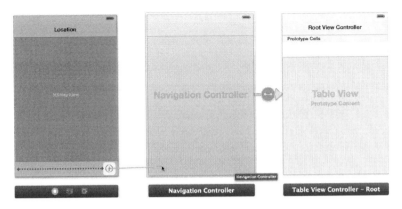

Figure 9.10 Create a segue from the Info button to the new Navigation Controller scene.

3. Let go of the mouse to display the Action Segue popup. This time select **modal** from the popup. Choosing the **modal** option creates a slightly different segue than you have seen so far. As you can see in Figure 9.11, the segue contains a small white rectangle.

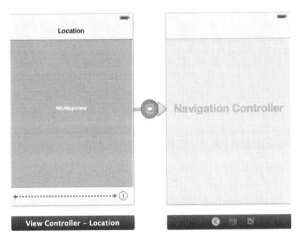

Figure 9.11 The new modal segue

4. Select the segue in the design surface and go to the Attributes Inspector. The **Transition** attribute specifies the type of aniation used to present the modal view. The **Default** option is the same as **Cover Vertical**, which specifies that the view slides up from the bottom of the screen. This is exactly what we want, so you can leave the attribute set to **Default**.

Setting Up the Map Options Scene

Now you're ready to configure the new Map Options scene. The options on this scene won't be functional for the prototype app. However, as with other scenes, this work is not "throw away." You can implement these options when converting the prototype to a real app.

1. Select the **MainStoryboard.storyboard** file in the Project Navigator.

2. Double-click the navigation bar in the Map Options scene (it's currently labeled **Root View Controller**). Change the title to **Map Options** (Figure 9.12) and press **Return**.

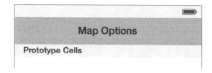

Figure 9.12 The Map Options navigation bar

3. Click in the gray area of the scene labeled **Table View Prototype Content** to select the table view. Next, go to the Attributes Inspector and change the following attributes:

   • **Content** to **Static Cells**.

   • **Style** to **Grouped**.

   • **Separator** to **Single Line**.

   When you're finished, the table view should look like Figure 9.13.

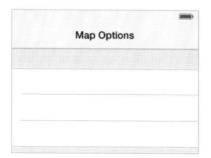

Figure 9.13 The updated Map Options table view

4. We need to add more section to the table view, but before doing this, you need to delete the last two rows in the table view. To do this, click on the second row to select it, hold down the **Shift** key, and then click on the third row to select it. Afterwards, press the **Delete** key, and you should have just one row remaining.

5. Next, select the table view by clicking in the gray area labeled **Table View**

Static Content. Go to the Attributes Inspector, and in the **Sections** attribute, click the up arrow once to create a total of two sections (Figure 9.14). We will create the other sections in just a bit.

Figure 9.14 The Map Options table view with two sections

6. In the Object Library, scroll near the top of the library, select the **Segmented Control**, and drag it to the first row of the Map Options table view. Position the segmented control so you see the horizontal guide line in the middle of the row, as well as the vertical guide line in the middle of the row (Figure 9.15), and then let go of the mouse button.

Figure 9.15 Positioning the segmented control

7. Let's add one more button to the segmented control. To do this, go to the Attributes Inspector and change the **Segments** value to **3** by clicking its up arrow. This adds a third button with no title.

8. Let's resize the segmented control so it fills up most of the cell. To do this, click on the small, square resizing handle on the left of the control and drag towards the left of the cell until you see the vertical guide line shown in Figure 9.16. Afterwards, grab the resize handle on the right side of the control and drag it to the right until you see the vertical guide line.

Figure 9.16 Resize the segmented control.

9. Now change the title of each button to the following values. Just double-click

the button to put its title into edit mode:

- Standard

- Satellite

- Hybrid

When you are finished, the buttons should look like Figure 9.17.

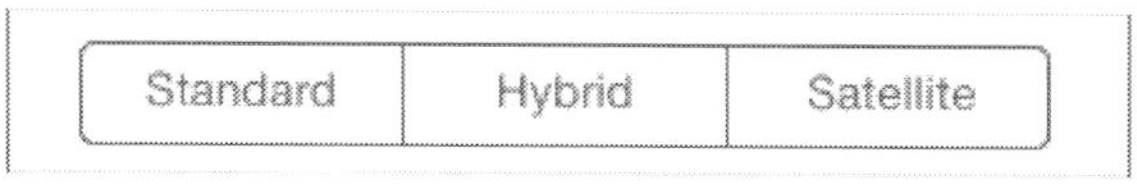

| Standard | Hybrid | Satellite |

Figure 9.17 The completed segmented control

10. All of the other rows in the table view are of the same style, so we'll set up the style of one cell and make copies of it.

   Click on the second cell in the table view to select it, and then go to the Attributes Inspector and set the **Style** attribute to **Basic**. This adds a **Title** label to the left side of the cell (Figure 9.18).

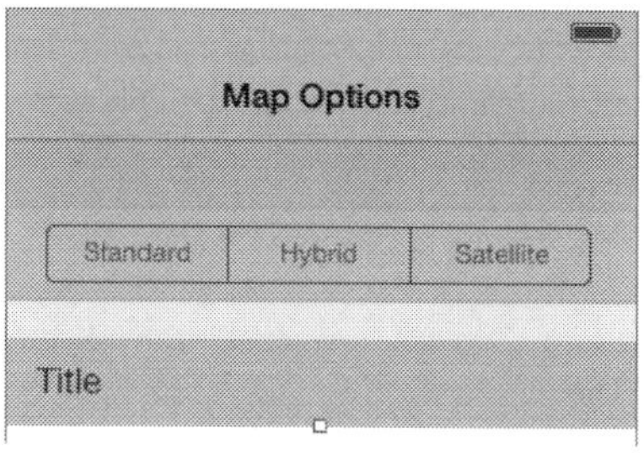

Map Options

| Standard | Hybrid | Satellite |

Title

*Figure 9.18 Set the second cell's **Style** to **Basic**.*

11. Click the cell twice to select the label contained within the cell, and then go to the Attributes Inspector and set the following attributes:

- **Font Size** to **16**.

- **Alignment** to **Center**.

12. Now let's change the text color of the label. To do this, click the double=headed arrow to the right of the **Color** attribute and in the color list, select **Other...** (Figure 9.19).

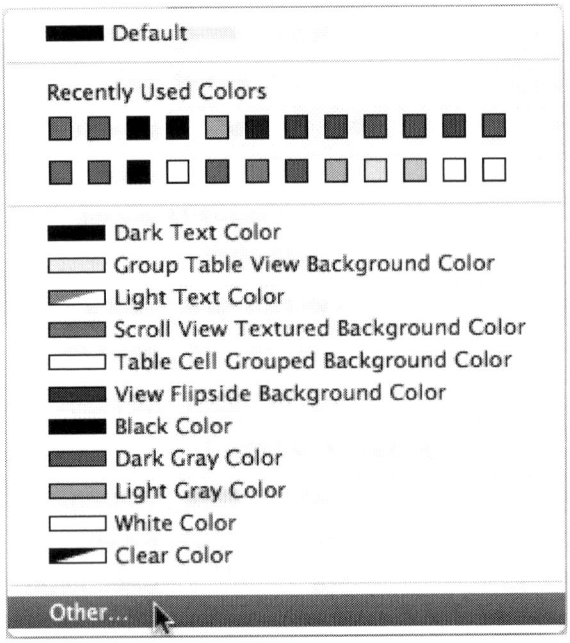

Figure 9.19 The color list

This displays the Color dialog (Figure 9.20).

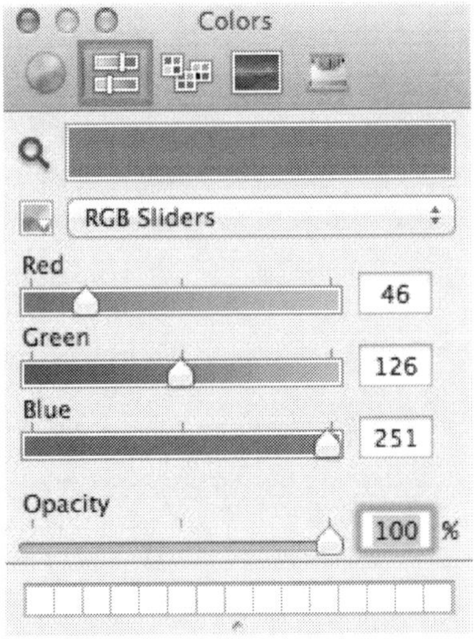

Figure 9.20 The Color dialog

13. The Color dialog has four different modes. To display the RGB sliders, click the second button from the left at the top of the Color dialog (Figure 9.20). Afterwards, change the RGB values by entering the following numbers in the text box associated with each color:

   • Red – 46

- Green – 126

- Blue – 251

14. This changes the text color of the label to the blue color shown in Figure 9.21.

Figure 19.21 The text color is set to blue.

15. Now that you have created the basic style for all other cells in this table view, let's add two more sections to the table view.

    To do this, select the table view by clicking in the gray area below the table view labeled **Table View Static Content**. Next, go to the Attributes Inspector and change the number of sections to **4** by clicking the up arrow twice in the **Sections** setting. When you're finished, the table view should look like Figure 9.22.

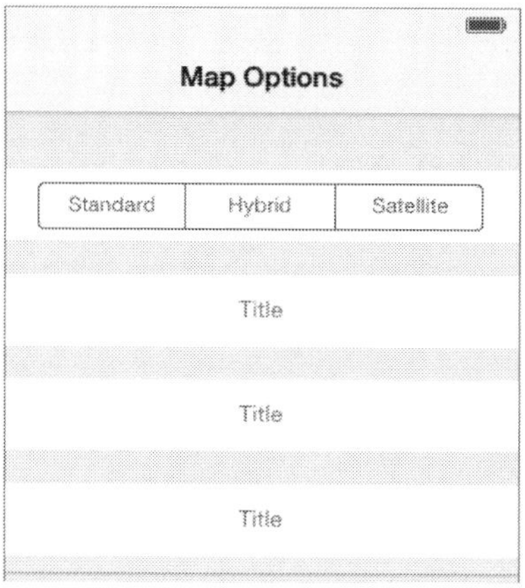

*Figure 9.22 Four sections in the **Map Options** table view*

16. We need one more cell in the second section of the table view. To create this, click on the second cell in the table view (the one below the cell that contains the segmented control) and press **Command+D**. This adds a second cell to the second section as shown in Figure 9.23.

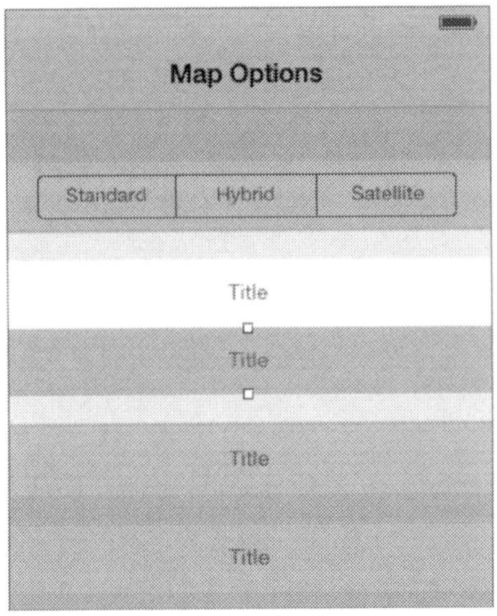

Figure 9.23 Add a second cell to the second section.

17. To finish up the table view, all you need to do is change the text of each label as shown in Figure 9.24. Just double-click each cell to put it into edit mode and then enter the text.

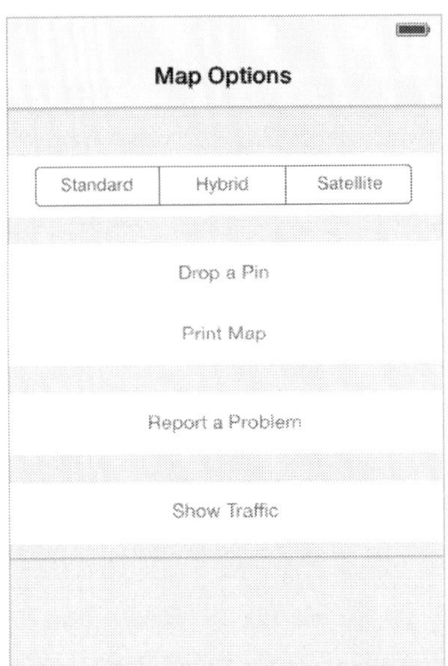

Figure 9.24 The completed **Map Options** table view

Adding a Done Button

The only task left on the Map Options scene is to add a **Done** button on the right side of the navigation bar.

1. Drag a **Bar Button Item** from the Object Library and hover it over the right side of the navigation bar. When you see the rounded rectangle appear

(Figure 9.25), release your mouse button.

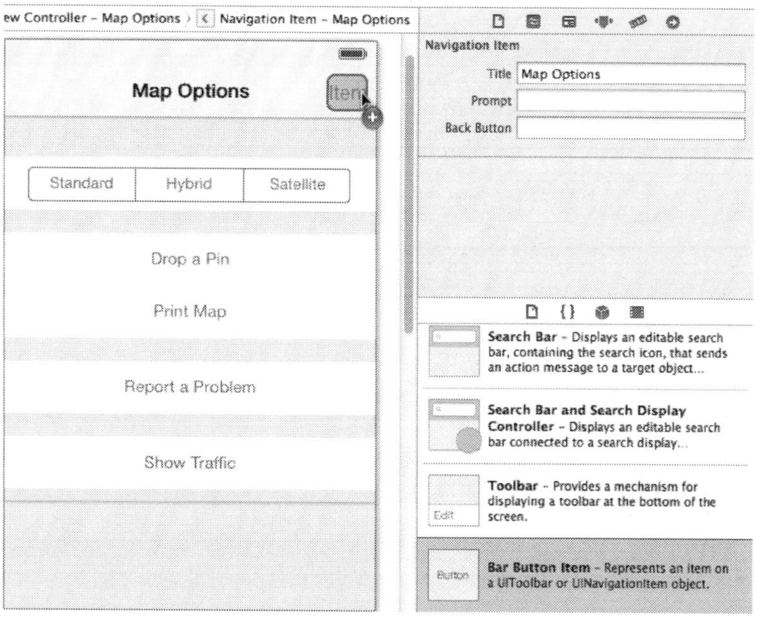

Figure 9.25 Add a **Bar Button Item** to the navigation bar.

2. Go to the Attributes Inspector and set the **Style** and **Identifier** attributes to **Done** (Figure 9.26).

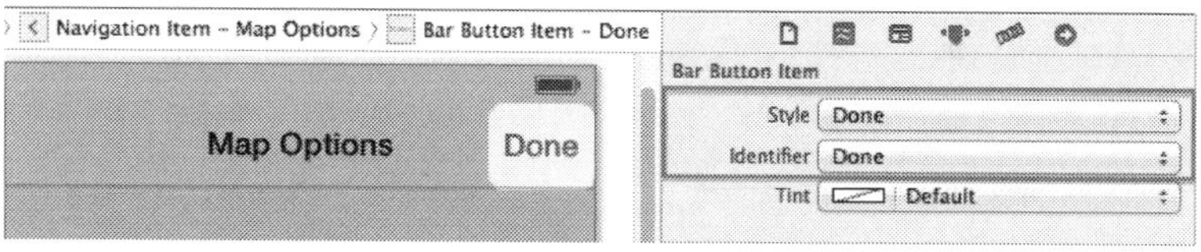

Figure 9.26 Set the **Style** and **Identifier** to **Done**.

When this scene gets converted from a prototype to a fully-functional app, tapping the **Done** button will dismiss the modal Map Options view. Unfortunately, you have to write code to make this happen, so for now, tapping the **Done** button won't do anything.

Testing the Map Options Scene

Now let's see how the Map Options scene looks at run time.

1. Click the **Run** button in Xcode.

2. After several seconds you should see the **Deliveries** scene. Select the first delivery in the list to see the **Shipment** scene.

Select the **Address** row to see **Location** scene, and then click the Info button at the bottom-right corner of the screen. You should see the **Map Options** scene (Figure 9.27) slide up from the bottom of the screen.

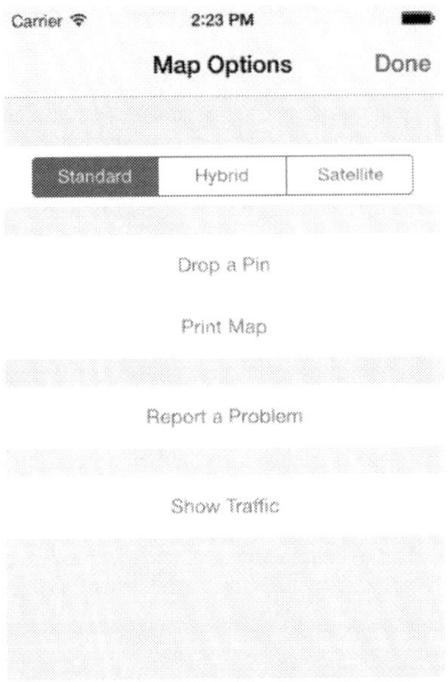

Figure 9.27 The completed Map Options scene

3. Again, since the Done button is not functional, you must go back to Xcode and press the **Stop** button to stop the app from running in the Simulator.

This completes the setup of the Map Options scene. I think you will find it's pretty fun to try different animations like this and see them at work in an app you have built that is running in the Simulator.

Summary

- You can use the Toolbar user-interface control to add a toolbar to scenes in your app.

- You can add a Flexible Space Bar Button Item to place toolbar buttons in the desired location on a toolbar.

- Creating a modal segue does not add a navigation bar to the top of the scene to which you are navigating.

- To add a navigation bar to a modal scene, add a Navigation Controller to the storyboard and create a segue to the Navigation Controller.

- In iOS, a modal window is usually a "dead end." The user transitions to a modal scene and back again, but the modal scene doesn't take you to another new scene.

- There are a few different transitions you can choose from when creating a modal segue.

- A segmented control groups two or more buttons together and provides a few different built-in styles to choose from.

Step-By-Step Movie 9.1

In case you missed any of the steps along the way, go to the following link in your web browser to see each step performed for you.

http://www.iOSAppsForNonProgrammers.com/B1M91.7.html

Conclusion

Now that you have created your first prototype app, what is your next step? Where do you go from here?

Where Do You Go From Here?

The main purpose of this book is to help you, the non-programmer feel a measure of confidence that building iOS apps *is* within your grasp. There's nothing like success to build confidence, and we hope you have found that confidence here.

So, what is your next step in learning to create iOS apps for the iPhone, iPad and iPod Touch?

The next step is learning the Objective-C programming language. This is something you need to embrace. In order to write apps, you need to learn a programming language. The next book in this series, *iOS App Development for Non-Programmers - Book 2: Flying With Objective-C*, takes the fear out of the whole process and makes it possible for you to learn how to write code.

Again, this second book was written specifically for non-programmers—those of you who have never written a line of code (or very little). We had numerous beta readers go through this book to make sure we explained concepts in a way that someone unfamiliar with programming terminology and techniques can understand.

There are also many exercises, interactive diagrams and videos to help you along the way. We find there's nothing quite like watching someone else write code to learn how to write code yourself!

You can do this!

Ask Questions on Our Forum!

To get answers to your questions and engage with others like yourself, check out our forum:

http://iOSAppsForNonProgrammers.com/forum

Training Classes

I regularly teach hands-on training classes (with small class sizes) where you can learn more about iOS app development in a friendly, in-person environment. For more information, check out our web site:

www.iOSAppsForNonProgrammers.com/training.html

Glossary

Activity Viewer   The Activity Viewer is an area at the top center of the Xcode window that displays status messages, project build warnings and errors, as well as the progress of tasks currently executing.

Animation   An animation is a smooth transition from one user-interface state to another; for example, when the user taps a button and one view slides out and another view slides in.

App   An app is a relatively small software application designed to perform one or more related tasks. In the context of this book, an app is specifically a software application that runs on an iPhone, iPod Touch or iPad.

Attribute   Attributes describe the characteristics of an object. Xcode's Attributes Inspector allows you to view and change the attributes of user-interface objects.

Build   When Xcode builds a project, it examines all the files in the project for errors and, if all is well, creates a single app file that can be run in Xcode's Simulator or on an actual iOS device.

Bundle identifier   The bundle identifier is Apple's way of uniquely identifying your app. By default, it is comprised of your company identifier and product name joined together.

Cocoa Touch Framework   The Cocoa Touch Framework is a set of many smaller frameworks (which contain sets of classes) each focusing on a set of core functionality that provides access to important services such as multi-touch gestures, user-interface controls, saving and retrieving data, user location, maps, camera, and compass.

Concatenate   Concatenate refers to the process of joining two strings together end-to-end.

Core logic   The core logic is the code in an app required to perform actions when a user-interface object is touched or any other processing takes place automatically. Whenever an app "does something," it requires code to execute a set of instructions.

Data   Data is the information and preferences maintained by an app. This can be as simple as storing the user's zip code or as complex as storing large amounts of data such as thousands of pictures and songs.

Disclosure indicator   A disclosure indicator is an arrow on the right side of a table view cell that indicates to the user that touching the row displays a screen with additional information.

Interface Builder   The Interface Builder editor is located in the center area of the Xcode window and allows you to lay out the user interface of your app.

iOS   See **Operating System**.

Navigation bar   A navigation bar is located at the top of a scene or view that is managed by a navigation controller. It contains a back button as well as other optional buttons you can add and customize.

Navigation Controller   A navigation controller is responsible for managing the navigation between different scenes, or views. It presents a navigation bar at the top of the screen, which contains a back button as well as other optional buttons you can add and customize.

Operating System   On an iOS device, iOS is the operating system. It is the software provided by Apple that manages the device hardware and provides the core functionality for all apps running on the device.

Processor   A processor is a central processing unit, or CPU. It is the hardware within a device that carries out programming instructions. For example, the iPhone 4 and iPad use the Apple A4 processor, the iPhone 4s and iPad 2 use the newer Apple A5 processor, and the New iPad uses the A5x processor.

Run time   Run time is when an app is running in the Simulator or on an iOS device.

Scene   Each iPhone screen on the storyboard is known as a scene.

Scene dock   The dark rectangular area below the scene is known as the scene dock. It contains an icon on the left that represents the first responder (the object with which the user is currently interacting). The icon on the right represents the view controller associated with the view.

Segue   A segue is a visual object in a storyboard that defines transitions between different scenes. A segue allows you to specify the UI control that fires the transition, the type of transition (sliding, curling, dissolving), and the scene that is moved into place as the new current view.

Storyboard   A storyboard is a design surface on which you can create a visual representation of your app's user interface. It allows you to lay out your app's user interface and navigation in a graphical, user-friendly way.

Table view   A table view is a user-interface control used to display lists of data in iOS apps. Each item in the table view is a row and a table view can contain an unlimited number of rows.

Table view cell   A table view cell is a user-interface control contained within a table view that you set up at design time. At run time, table view rows are created from table view cell definitions.

Table view controller   A table view controller is responsible for displaying an associated table view at run time, filling the table view with data and responding to the user interacting with the table view.

Table view row   A table view row is a single item listed in a table view at run time. A row is one column wide and can contain an image, text, and an accessory icon such as the disclosure indicator. A table view row at run time is created from a table view cell that you configure at design time.

Table view section   Each division of a table view is a section. If you have no divisions, you have only one section.

UI   UI is an acronym for User Interface.

User Interface   The user interface is the part of the app that the user sees and interacts with by touch. It includes buttons, text fields, lists, and, as is the case with many games, the entire touch-screen surface.

View   A view contains one screen of information on an iOS device.

View Controller   Every view in an iOS app has a **view controller** that works behind the scenes in conjunction with the view.

It has properties that, (among other things)

- Indicate if the user can edit items in the view,

- Report the orientation of the user interface (portrait or landscape), and

- Allow you to access user-interface elements.

It has methods that:

- Allow you to navigate to other views,

- Specify the interface orientations that the view supports, and

- Indicate when the associated view is loaded and unloaded from the screen.

View controller objects are based on the Cocoa Touch Framework's **UIViewController** class, or one of its subclasses.

Xcode   Xcode is Apple's free software development tool. You can use it to create iOS apps or Mac desktop apps.

About the Author

So, I was supposed to be a hardware guy.

While I was in college majoring in electronic engineering, I worked at a small company as I paid my way through school. Brian, the head of the software department, would tell me on a regular basis "You know, I think you're a software guy!"

Hardware guys typically do *not* want to be software guys, so I just ignored it as good-natured harassment. Then one day I decided to get him off my back by giving it a try.

As they say, the rest is history. I fell in love with writing software, and the honeymoon is definitely not over!

I learned that writing software is a *very* creative process. In just a matter of hours, I could conceive an idea, create a software design and have it up and running on a computer.

The first software I wrote was a tutorial program that helped new computer users understand how a computer works (this was not long after the birth of the PC). I came up with the idea after watching new computer users give up on themselves before they started.

Since then, I've devoted my teaching career to making difficult concepts easy to understand. So, when Apple released the iPhone and a platform for building apps, I immediately started teaching classes to empower others to join this software revolution and share in the fun. Maybe you'll find you're a software "guy" too. — Kevin

Books in This Series by Kevin McNeish

1. *Book 1: Diving Into iOS*

2. *Book 2: Flying With Objective-C*

3. *Book 3: Navigating Xcode*

4. *More books coming soon!*

Questions and Comments for the Author

Email me at:

kevin@iOSAppsForNonProgrammers.com

Training Classes

I regularly teach hands-on training classes (with small class sizes) where you can learn more about iOS app development in a friendly, in-person environment. For more information, check out our web site:

www.iOSAppsForNonProgrammers.com/training.html

Rate and Recommend This Book

If you have enjoyed this book and think it's worth telling others about, please leave your comments and rating for this book on our Amazon book page and tell your friends. Thanks!

Printed in Great Britain
by Amazon.co.uk, Ltd.,
Marston Gate.